POETRY FOR PLEASURE

POETRY
FOR PLEASURE

A Choice of Poetry & Verse
On a Variety of Themes

Made by
IAN PARSONS
and illustrated by
JOHN WARD RA

1977
CHATTO & WINDUS
LONDON

Published by
Chatto & Windus Ltd
40 William IV Street
London WC2N 4DF

*

Clarke, Irwin & Co
Toronto

British Library Cataloguing in Publication Data

Poetry for pleasure.
    1. English poetry
    Ian Parsons,
    821'.008   PR1174
    ISBN 0-7011-2279-X

Printed in Great Britain by
Redwood Burn Limited
Trowbridge & Esher

For T.R.
With love

ACKNOWLEDGMENTS

My first debt of gratitude must be to Norah Smallwood, whose idea this anthology originally was, who encouraged me to persevere with it, and who designed it herself.

Grateful thanks are also due to the following for their kind permission to reprint the copyright poems included in this volume:

Punch for the poem by Patrick Barrington; Nicholas Bentley for poems by E. C. Bentley: to A. D. Peters & Co. for the poem by Edmund Blunden; Oxford University Press for poems from *The Poetical Works of Robert Bridges*; the Executors of his Estate for poems from *Adamaster* by Roy Campbell; the Executors of his Estate, Jonathan Cape & The Hogarth Press for the poems by C. Day Lewis; the Literary Trustees of Walter de la Mare, and The Society of Authors as their representative, for poems from *The Complete Poems of Walter de la Mare, 1969*; Faber & Faber Ltd. for the poems by T. S. Eliot from *Old Possum's Book of Practical Cats*, the poem from *The Collected Poems of Louis MacNeice*, and the poem by Edwin Muir from *Collected Poems*; Edward Arnold Ltd. for the poem by Harry Graham from *Most Ruthless Rhymes For Heartless Homes*; Methuen & Co. & Charles Scribner's Sons for the poem by Kenneth Grahame from *The Wind in the Willows*. Text copyright University Chest Oxford; the Trustees of the Hardy Estate and Macmillan London and Canada for the poems by Thomas Hardy from *Collected Poems*; George Allen & Unwin for the poem by Ralph Hodgson from *The Last Blackbird*; the Society of Authors as the literary representative of the Estate of A. E. Housman and Jonathan Cape for poems by A. E. Housman from *Collected Poems*; the National Trust and Methuen & Co. for *A Drifter Off Tarentum* from *Epitaphs* by Rudyard Kipling; the National Trust and Macmillan & Co. of London for the poems from *The Definitive Edition of Rudyard Kipling's Verse*; Laurence Pollinger Ltd. and the Estate of the late Mrs. Frieda Lawrence for poems from *The Complete Poems of D. H. Lawrence*; the Executors of her Estate and Jonathan Cape for the poem by Lillian Bowes Lyon; Nigel Nicolson for the poem by V. Sackville-West; George Sassoon and Faber & Faber for the poems by Siegfried Sassoon; J. M. Dent & Sons and the Trustees for the Copyrights of the late Dylan Thomas for the poem from *Collected Poems*; M. B. Yeats, Miss Anne Yeats and the Macmillan Co. of London for poems from *The Collected Poems of W. B. Yeats*.

TO THE READER

Making an anthology of any kind is a high-risk undertaking. For it involves choosing, and the chances of any one individual's choice coinciding closely with that of his readers are remote. This is particularly true of poetry, where the field of choice is so wide, and the judgements that have to be made so inescapably subjective. Dissent, both as to inclusions and exclusions, is inevitable. But at least the compiler can try to explain what his book is about, how it is organised, and what it sets out to do.

To describe what this particular anthology is about it will be quickest and simplest to say briefly what it is *not*. First then, it makes no claim to be a comprehensive selection of English verse, or to mirror any particular period, or to represent any specific category of poetry – such as humorous verse or ballads. The existence of the classic Oxford Books of Verse makes any such undertaking superfluous.

Secondly, in order to keep the length – which in turn governs the price – of the book within bounds, I have set myself certain limits. Thus I have included nothing written earlier than the 16th Century, and nothing by living poets. And I have confined my choice to the work of British writers, though I have stretched a point in the case of T. S. Eliot on the grounds that he spent the greater part of his working life in England, and is buried here.

The book is arranged in sections, each of which covers, but only in broad outline, a specific theme or group of related themes. For example, the Section entitled *Behold Mortality* includes poems about Time, Age, and Sleep, as well as Death. It proved impossible to find a title for each Section that was accurately inclusive without being cumbrous, but I hope the results are sufficiently self-explanatory. The book opens with two or three Sections devoted to verse written for or about the young and the very young, and then moves on into the realm of adult poetry. The subsequent sequence of themes is purely personal, and the contents of each Section are themselves necessarily arbitrary, since many of the major poems I have included span a number of different themes. Such poems will be familiar to the majority of readers, and I make no apology for that; an anthology composed entirely of unknown or little-known work is apt to alarm rather than attract. At the same time, I would hope that a fair proportion of the contents will be new to many.

Finally, I need hardly say that the book does not set out to reflect any particular philosophy of life, still less to promote any doctrine or creed. Its sole object, as the title implies, is to give pleasure. I hope it will.

I.M.P.

CONTENTS

LIST OF AUTHORS

BELLS ACROSS THE SAND

Weep not, my wanton, smile upon my knee;
When thou art old there's grief enough for thee
ROBERT GREENE

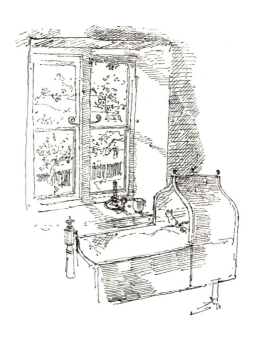

INFANT SORROW

My mother groan'd, my father wept,
Into the dangerous world I leapt;
Helpless, naked, piping loud,
Like a fiend hid in a cloud.

Struggling in my father's hands,
Striving against my swaddling-bands,
Bound and weary, I thought best
To sulk upon my mother's breast.

William Blake

LULLABY

Love me — I love you,
  Love me, my baby;
Sing it high, sing it low,
  Sing it as may be.

Mother's arms under you;
  Her eyes above you;
Sing it high, sing it low,
  Love me — I love you.

Christina Rossetti

DARBY AND JOAN

Darby and Joan are dressed in black,
Sword and buckler behind their back;
Foot to foot and knee to knee,
Turn again Darby's company.

Anon.

MY FATHER DIED

My father died a month ago,
He left me all his riches —
A feather bed and a wooden leg,
And a pair of calico breeches;
A coffee-pot without a spout,
A cup without a handle,
A baccy-box without a lid,
And half a ha'penny candle.

Anon.

SWEET CAROLINE

Sweet, sweet Caroline,
Dipt her face in Turpentine,
Turpentine made it shine,
Sweet, sweet Caroline.

Anon.

CAROLINE PINK

Caroline Pink, she fell down the sink,
She caught the Scarlet Fever,
Her husband had to leave her,
She called in Doctor Blue,
And he caught it too —
Caroline Pink from China Town.

Anon.

POP GOES THE WEASEL

Up and down the City road,
   In and out the Eagle;
That's the way the money goes,
   Pop goes the weasel.

Half a pound o'tuppenny rice,
   Half a pound o'treacle;
That's the way the money goes,
   Pop goes the weasel.

A penny for a cotton ball,
   A ha'penny for a needle;
That's the way the money goes,
   Pop goes the weasel.

and here's another verse from Scotland:

My wee boy's a bonny wee boy,
   Your wee boy's a deevil;
That's the way the money goes,
   Pop goes the weasel!

Anon.

OUT GOES SHE

Up in the North, a long way off,
The donkey's got the whooping-cough.
Penny on the water, tuppence on the sea,
Threepence on the railway — out goes she.

Anon.

HI, HI, CURLYWIG

I went down the lane to buy a
   penny whistle,
A copper came by and pinched my
   penny whistle.
I asked him for it back, he said he
   hadn't got it —
Hi, Hi, Curlywig, you've got it in
   your pocket.

Anon.

TWO GRACES

I

Here a little child I stand,
Heaving up my either hand;
Cold as Paddocks though they be,
Here I lift them up to Thee,
For a Benison to fall
On our meat, and on us all. *Amen*

II

What God gives, and what we take,
'Tis a gift for Christ His sake.
Be the meal of beans and pease,
God be thanked for those and these.
Have we flesh, or have we fish,
All are fragments from His dish.

Robert Herrick

THE BELLS OF LONDON

Gay go up and gay go down,
To ring the bells of London town.

Oranges and lemons,
Say the bells of St. Clement's.

Pancakes and fritters,
Say the bells of St. Peter's.

Two sticks and an apple,
Say the bells of Whitechapel.

Kettles and pans,
Say the bells of St. Ann's.

Halfpence and farthings,
Say the bells of St. Martin's.

You owe me ten shillings,
Say the bells of St. Helen's.

When will you pay me?
Say the bells of Old Bailey.

When I grow rich,
Say the bells of Shoreditch.

Pray when will that be?
Say the bells of Stepney.

I am sure I don't know,
Says the great bell at Bow.

Here comes a candle to light you to bed,
Here comes a chopper to chop off your head.

Anon.

PEAS AND HONEY

I always eat peas with honey,
I've done it all my life;
It makes the peas taste funny,
But it keeps them on the knife.

Anon.

THREE RIDDLES

As soft as silk, as white as milk,
As bitter as gall, a thick wall
And a green coat over me all.

A Walnut

Every lady in the land
Has twenty nails upon each hand
Five and twenty on hands and feet;
All this is true without deceit.

Try putting a comma after 'nails'

In marble halls as white as milk,
Lined with a skin as soft as silk,
Within a fountain crystal-clear
A golden apple doth appear.
No doors there are to this stronghold,
Yet thieves break in and steal the gold.

An Egg

Anon.

DAWLISH FAIR

Over the Hill and over the Dale,
And over the Bourne to Dawlish,
Where ginger-bread wives have a scanty sale,
And ginger-bread nuts are smallish.

John Keats

RANSI—TANSI—TAY

Here come three dukes a-riding,
    a-riding, a-riding,
Here come three dukes a-riding
    with a Ransi-tansi-tay.

Please we've come to marry,
    to marry, to marry,
Please we've come to marry
    with a Ransi-tansi-tay.

Marry one of us Sir.
    us Sir, us Sir,
Marry one of us Sir
    with a Ransi-tansi-tay.

You're all as stiff as pokers,
    as pokers, as pokers,
You're all as stiff as pokers
    with a Ransi-tansi-tay.

We can bend as well as you Sir,
    you Sir, you Sir,
We can bend as well as you Sir
    with a Ransi-tansi-tay.

You're all too black and dirty,
    dirty, dirty,
You're all too black and dirty
    with a Ransi-tansi-tay!

Anon.

ALGY MET A BEAR

Algy met a bear,
A bear met Algy,
The bear was bulgy,
The bulge was Algy.

Anon.

THREE YOUNG RATS

Three young rats with black felt hats,
　　Three young ducks with white straw flats,
　　　Three young dogs with curling tails,
　　　　Three young cats with demi-veils,
　　　　　　Went out to walk with two young pigs
　　　　　　In satin vests and sorrel wigs;
　　But suddenly it chanced to rain,
　　And so they all went home again.

Anon.

THE KEEL ROW

As I came through Sandgate,
　　Through Sandgate, through Sandgate,
As I came through Sandgate
　　I heard a lassie sing,
O weel may the keel row,
The keel row, the keel row;
O weel may the keel row,
　　That my laddie's in.

O wha's like my Johnny,
Sae leith, sae blythe, sae bonny?
He's foremost among the mony
　　Keel lads o'coaly Tyne:
He'll set and row so tightly,
Or in the dance — so sprightly —
He'll cut and shuffle sightly;
　　'Tis true, — were he not mine.

He wears a blue bonnet,
Blue bonnet, blue bonnet;
He wears a blue bonnet,
　　And a dimple in his chin:
And weel may the keel row,
The keel row, the keel row;
And weel may the keel row,
　　That my laddie's in.

Anon.

WASH WELL THE FRESH FISH

Wash well the fresh fish, wash well the fresh fish,
Wash well the fresh fish,
   And skim well the bree;
For there's many a foul-footed thing, many a foul-
   footed thing,
     Many a foul-footed thing
      In the salt sea.

Anon.

THE ANIMAL FAIR

I went to the animal fair
The birds and the beasts were there,
The great baboon
By the light of the moon
Was combing his auburn hair.
The monkey he got drunk,
And sat on the elephant's trunk,
The elephant sneezed
And fell on his knees
And what became of the
   monkey-monkey-monk?

Anon.

A DIS, A DIS, A GREEN GRASS

A dis, a dis, a green grass,
   A dis, a dis, a dis;
Come all you pretty fair maids
   And dance along with us.

For we are going roving,
   A roving in this land;
We take this pretty fair maid,
   We take her by the hand.

She shall get a duke, my dear,
 As duck do get a drake;
And she shall have a young prince,
 For her own fair sake.

                              Anon.

THE HERRING LOVES
THE MERRY MOONLIGHT

The herring loves the merry moonlight,
 The mackerel loves the wind;
But the oyster loves the dredging song,
 For she comes of a gentle kind.

                              Anon.

MY MOTHER SAID

My Mother said I never should
Play with the gipsies in the wood.
 The wood was dark; the grass was green;
 In came Sally with a tambourine.

I crept to the sea — no ship to get across;
I paid ten shillings for a blind white horse.
I up on his back and was off in a crack,
Sally, tell my Mother I shall never come back.

                              Anon.

21

DANCE TO YOUR DADDIE

Dance to your daddie,
  My bonnie laddie,
Dance to your daddie, my bonnie lamb!
  You shall get a fishie,
  On a little dishie,
You shall get a herring when the boat
  comes hame!

Dance to your daddie,
  My bonnie laddie,
Dance to your daddie, and to your mammie
  sing!
  You shall get a coatie,
  And a pair of breekies,
You shall get a coatie when the boat comes in!

Anon.

HERE WE COME A-PIPING

Here we come a-piping,
In Springtime and in May;
Green fruit a-ripening,
And Winter fled away.
The Queen she sits upon the strand,
Fair as lily, white as wand;
Seven billows on the sea,
Horses riding fast and free,
And bells across the sand.

Anon.

22

END OF TERM

To-night, to-night,
The pillow fight,
To-morrow's the end of school;
Break the dishes, break the chairs,
And trip the teachers on the stairs!

Anon.

2

THE HARP OF YOUTH

In delay there lies no plenty;
Then come kiss me, sweet and twenty,
Youth's a stuff will not endure

SHAKESPEARE

EIGHT O'CLOCK BELLS

Eight o'clock bells are ringing,
Mother may I go out?
My young man's a-waiting
For to take me out.
First he bought me apples,
Then he bought me pears,
Then he gave me sixpence
To kiss him on the stairs.

Anon.

LILIES ARE WHITE

Lilies are white,
Rosemary's green;
When you are king,
I will be queen.

Roses are red,
Lavender's blue;
If you will have me,
I will have you.

Anon.

OH! DEAR!

Oh! dear! what can the matter be?
Dear! dear! what can the matter be?
Oh! dear! what can the matter be?
Johnny's so long at the fair.

He promised he'd buy me a fairing should please me,
And then for a kiss, oh! he vowed he would tease me,
He promised he'd bring me a bunch of blue ribbons
To tie up my bonny brown hair.

And it's oh! dear! what can the matter be?
Dear! dear! what can the matter be?
Oh! dear! what can the matter be?
Johnny's so long at the fair.

He promised he'd bring me a basket of posies,
A garland of lilies, a garland of roses,
A little straw hat, to set off the blue ribbons
That tie up my bonny brown hair.

And it's oh! dear! what can the matter be?
Dear! dear! what can the matter be?
Oh! dear! what can the matter be?
Johnny's so long at the fair.

Anon.

ALL ON A SUMMER'S DAY

Oh, what is Jeanie weeping for,
A-weeping for, a-weeping for,
Oh, what is Jeanie weeping for,
All on this summer's day?

I'm weeping for my own true love,
My own true love, my own true love;
I'm weeping for my own true love,
All on this summer's day.

Rise up and choose another love,
Another love, another love,
Rise up and choose another love,
All on this summer's day.

Anon.

SISTER, AWAKE!

Sister, awake! close not your eyes,
    The day her light discloses,
And the bright morning doth arise
    Out of her bed of roses.

See the clear sun, the world's bright eye,
    In at our window peeping:
Lo, how he blusheth to espy
    Us idle wenches sleeping!

Therefore awake! make haste, I say,
    And let us, without staying,
All in our gowns of green so gay
    Into the park a-maying.

Anon.

DOWN IN YONDER MEADOW

Down in yonder meadow where the green grass grows,
Pretty Pollie Pillicote bleaches her clothes.
She sang, she sang, she sang, oh, so sweet,
She sang, Oh, come over! across the street.

He kissed her, he kissed her, he bought her a gown,
A gown of rich cramasie out of the town.
He bought her a gown and a guinea gold ring,
A guinea, a guinea, a guinea gold ring.

Up street, and down, shine the windows made of glass,
Oh, isn't Pollie Pillicote a braw young lass?
Cherries in her cheeks, and ringlets her hair,
Hear her singing Handy Dandy up and down the stair.

Anon.

OUR VISIT TO THE ZOO

When we went to the Zoo
We saw a gnu,
   An elk and a whelk
And a wild emu.

We saw a hare
And a bear in his lair,
   And a seal have a meal
On a high-backed chair.

We saw a snake
That was hardly awake,
   And a lion eat meat
They'd forgotten to bake.

We saw a coon
And a baby baboon.
   The giraffe made us laugh
All afternoon!

We saw a crab
And a long-tailed dab,
   And we all went home
In a taxi-cab.

Jessie Pope

I LOVED A LASS

I loved a lass, a fair one,
   As fair as e'er was seen;
She was indeed a rare one,
   Another Sheba Queen:
But, fool as then I was,
   I thought she loved me too:
But now, alas! she's left me,
   Falero, lero, loo!

28

Her hair like gold did glister,
   Each eye was like a star,
She did·surpass her sister,
   Which pass'd all others far;
She would me honey call,
   She'd — O she'd kiss me too!
But now, alas! she's left me,
   Falero, lero, loo!

Many a merry meeting
   My love and I have had;
She was my only sweeting,
   She made my heart full glad;
The tears stood in her eyes
   Like to the morning dew:
But now, alas! she's left me,
   Falero, lero, loo!

Her cheeks were like the cherry,
   Her skin was white as snow;
When she was blithe and merry
   She angel-like did show;
Her waist exceeding small,
   The fives did fit her shoe:
But now, alas! she's left me,
   Falero, lero, loo!

In summer time or winter
   She had her heart's desire;
I still did scorn to stint her
   From sugar, sack or fire;
The world went round about,
   No cares we ever knew:
But now, alas! she's left me,
   Falero, lero, loo!

To maidens' vows and swearing
  Henceforth no credit give;
You may give them the hearing,
  But never them believe;
They are as false as fair,
  Unconstant, frail, untrue:
For mine, alas! hath left me,
  Falero, lero, loo!

George Wither

BUDMOUTH DEARS

When we lay where Budmouth Beach is,
O, the girls were fresh as peaches,
With their tall and tossing figures and their eyes of blue and
  brown!
    And our hearts would ache with longing
    As we paced from our sing-songing,
With a smart *Clink! Clink!* up the Esplanade and down.

    They distracted and delayed us
    By the pleasant pranks they played us,
And what marvel, then, if troopers, even of regiments of
  renown,
    On whom flashed those eyes divine, O,
    Should forget the countersign, O,
As we tore *Clink! Clink!* back to camp above the town

    Do they miss us much, I wonder,
    Now that war has swept us sunder,
And we roam from where the faces smile to where the
  faces frown?
    And no more behold the features
    Of the fair fantastic creatures,
And no more *Clink! Clink!* past the parlours of the town?

Shall we once again there meet them?
  Falter fond attempts to greet them?
Will the gay sling-jacket glow again beside the muslin gown?
  Will they archly quiz and con us
  With a sideway glance upon us,
While our spurs *Clink! Clink!* up the Esplanade and down?

Thomas Hardy

From A SHROPSHIRE LAD

When I was one-and-twenty
  I heard a wise man say,
'Give crowns and pounds and guineas
  But not your heart away;
Give pearls away and rubies
  But keep your fancy free.'
But I was one-and-twenty,
  No use to talk to me.

When I was one-and-twenty
  I heard him say again,
'The Heart out of the bosom
  Was never given in vain;
'Tis paid with sighs a plenty
  And sold for endless rue.'
And I am two-and-twenty,
  And oh, 'tis true, 'tis true.

A E Housman

ONE—AND—TWENTY

Long expected one-and-twenty,
  Ling'ring year, at length is flown:
Pride and pleasure, pomp and plenty,
  Great . . ., are now your own.

Loosen'd from the minor's tether,
  Free to mortgage or to sell,
Wild as wind, and light as feather,
  Bid the sons of thrift farewell.

Call the Betsies, Kates, and Jennies,
  All the names that banish care;
Lavish of your grandsire's guineas,
  Show the spirit of an heir.

All that prey on vice and folly
  Joy to see their quarry fly:
There the gamester, light and jolly,
  There the lender, grave and sly.

Wealth, my lad, was made to wander,
  Let it wander as it will;
Call the jockey, call the pander,
  Bid them come and take their fill.

When the bonny blade carouses,
  Pockets full, and spirits high —
What are acres? What are houses?
  Only dirt, or wet or dry.

Should the guardian friend or mother
  Tell the woes of wilful waste,
Scorn their counsel, scorn their pother; —
  You can hang or drown at last!

Samuel Johnson

WEST WIND

West wind tae the bairn,
  When going for its name;
And rain tae the corpse,
Carried tae its lang hame.

A bonny blue sky,
Tae welcome the bride,
As she gangs tae the kirk,
With the sun on her side.

Anon.

⚜

THREE KNIGHTS FROM SPAIN

We are three Brethren come from Spain,
  All in French garlands;
We are come to court your daughter Jane,
  And adieu to you, my darlings.

My daughter Jane! — she is too young,
  All in French garlands;
She cannot bide your flattering tongue,
  And adieu to you, my darlings.

Be she young, or be she old,
  All in French garlands;
'Tis for a bride she must be sold,
  And adieu to you, my darlings.

A bride, a bride, she shall not be,
  All in French garlands;
Till she go through this world with me,
  And adieu to you, my darlings.

Then shall you keep your daughter Jane,
　　All in French garlands;
Come once, we come not here again,
　　And adieu to you, my darlings.

Turn back, turn back, you Spanish Knights,
　　All in French garlands;
Scour, scour your spurs, till they be bright,
　　And adieu to you, my darlings.

Sharp shine our spurs, all richly wrought,
　　All in French garlands;
In towns afar our spurs were bought,
　　And adieu to you, my darlings.

Smell my lilies, smell my roses,
　　All in French garlands;
Which of my maidens do you choose?
　　And adieu to you, my darlings.

Not she. Not she. Thy youngest, Jane!
　　All in French garlands;
We ride — and ride not back again,
　　And adieu to you, my darlings.

In every pocket a thousand pound,
　　All in French garlands;
On every finger a gay gold ring,
　　And adieu to you, my darlings.
　　And adieu to you, my darlings.

Anon.

SALLY IN OUR ALLEY

Of all the girls that are so smart
There's none like pretty Sally;
She is the darling of my heart,
And she lives in our alley.
There is no lady in the land
Is half so sweet as Sally;
She is the darling of my heart,
And she lives in our alley.

Her father he makes cabbage-nets,
And through the streets does cry 'em;
Her mother she sells laces long
To such as please to buy 'em:
But sure such folks could ne'er beget
So sweet a girl as Sally!
She is the darling of my heart,
And she lives in our alley.

When she is by, I leave my work,
I love her so sincerely;
My master comes like any Turk,
And bangs me most severely:
But let him bang his bellyful,
I'll bear it all for Sally;
She is the darling of my heart,
And she lives in our alley.

Of all the days that's in the week
I dearly love but one day —
And that's the day that comes betwixt
A Saturday and Monday;
For then I'm drest all in my best
To walk abroad with Sally;
She is the darling of my heart,
And she lives in our alley.

My master carries me to church,
And often am I blamèd
Because I leave him in the lurch
As soon as text is namèd;
I leave the church in sermon-time
And slink away to Sally;
She is the darling of my heart,
And she lives in our alley.

When Christmas comes about again,
O, then I shall have money;
I'll hoard it up, and box it all,
I'll give it to my honey:
I would it were ten thousand pound,
I'd give it all to Sally;
She is the darling of my heart,
And she lives in our alley.

My master and the neighbours all,
Make game of me and Sally,
And, but for her, I'd better be
A slave and row a galley;
But when my seven long years are out,
O, then I'll marry Sally;
O, then we'll wed, and then we'll bed —
But not in our alley!

Henry Carey

MYRA

I, with whose colours Myra dress'd her head,
   I, that ware posies of her own hand-making,
I, that mine own name in the chimneys read
   By Myra finely wrought ere I was waking:
Must I look on, in hope time coming may
With change bring back my turn again to play?

I, that on Sunday at the church-stile found
   A garland sweet with true-love-knots in flowers,
Which I to wear about mine arms was bound
   That each of us might know that all was ours:
Must I lead now an idle life in wishes,
And follow Cupid for his loaves and fishes?

I, that did wear the ring her mother left,
   I, for whose love she gloried to be blamèd,
I, with whose eyes her eyes committed theft,
   I, who did make her blush when I was namèd:
Must I lose ring, flowers, blush, theft, and go naked,
Watching with sighs till dead love be awakèd?

Was it for this that I might Myra see
   Washing the water with her beauty's white?
Yet would she never write her love to me.
   Thinks wit of change when thoughts are in delight?
Mad girls may safely love as they may leave;
No man can *print* a kiss: lines may deceive.

                            Fulke Greville

AH! SUN—FLOWER

Ah, Sun-flower! weary of time,
Who countest the steps of the sun;
Seeking after that sweet golden clime,
Where the traveller's journey is done;

Where the Youth pined away with desire,
And the pale Virgin shrouded in snow,
Arise from their graves, and aspire
Where my Sun-flower wishes to go.

                          William Blake

DELIGHT IN DISORDER

A sweet disorder in the dress
Kindles in clothes a wantonnes:
A lawn about the shoulders thrown
Into a fine distraction:
An erring lace, which here and there
Enthrals the crimson stomacher:
A cuff neglectful, and thereby
Ribbands to flow confusedly:
A winning wave, deserving note,
In the tempestuous petticoat:
A careless shoe-string, in whose tie
I see a wild civility:
Do more bewitch me than when art
Is too precise in every part.

Robert Herrick

'FROM YOU I HAVE BEEN ABSENT'

From you I have been absent in the spring,
When proud-pied April, dress'd in all his trim,
Hath put a spirit of youth in everything,
That heavy Saturn laugh'd and leap'd with him.
Yet nor the lays of birds, nor the sweet smell
Of different flowers in odour and in hue,
Could make me any summer's story tell,
Or from their proud lap pluck them where they grew;
Nor did I wonder at the Lily's white,
Nor praise the deep vermilion in the Rose;
They were but sweet, but figures of delight,
Drawn after you, you pattern of all those.
    Yet seem'd it Winter still, and, you away,
    As with your shadow I with these did play.

William Shakespeare

38

GO, LOVELY ROSE

Go, lovely Rose —
Tell her that wastes her time and me,
 That now she knows,
When I resemble her to thee,
How sweet and fair she seems to be.

 Tell her that's young,
And shuns to have her graces spied,
 That hadst thou sprung
In deserts where no men abide,
Thou must have uncommended died.

 Small is the worth
Of beauty from the light retired:
 Bid her come forth,
Suffer herself to be desired,
And not blush so to be admired.

 Then die — that she
The common fate of all things rare
 May read in thee;
How small a part of time they share
That are so wondrous sweet and fair!

Edmund Waller

SONNET

I must not grieve my Love, whose eyes would read
Lines of delight, whereon her youth might smile;
Flowers have time before they come to seed,
And she is young, and now must sport the while.
And sport, Sweet Maid, in season of these years,
And learn to gather flowers before they wither;
And where the sweetest blossom first appears,
Let Love and Youth conduct thy pleasures thither.
Lighten forth smiles to clear the clouded air,
And calm the tempest which my sighs do raise;
Pity and smiles do best become the fair;
Pity and smiles must only yield thee praise.
    Make me to say when all my griefs are gone,
    Happy the heart that sighed for such a one!

Samuel Daniel

3

BIRD, BEAST AND FLOWER

Mothers of large families who claim to common sense
Will find a Tiger will repay the trouble and expense

HILAIRE BELLOC

LITTLE JENNY WREN

Little Jenny Wren
Fell sick upon a time;
   In came Robin Redbreast,
      And brought her cake and wine.

   Eat of my cake, Jenny,
  And drink of my wine;
Thank you, Robin, kindly,
You shall be mine.

Jenny she got well,
And stood upon her feet,
   And told Robin plainly
      She loved him not a bit.
    Robin, he was angry,
  And hopped upon a twig,
Saying, out upon you, fie upon you,
    Bold-faced jig!

Anon.

THE FLY

How large unto the tiny fly
  Must little things appear!
A rosebud like a feather bed,
  Its prickle like a spear;

A dewdrop like a looking-glass,
  A hair like golden wire;
The smallest grain of mustard-seed
  As fierce as coals of fire;

A loaf of bread, a lofty hill;
  A wasp, a cruel leopard;
And specks of salt as bright to see
  As lambkins to a shepherd.

Walter de la Mare

THE TWO RATS

He was a rat, and she was a rat,
   And down in one hole they did dwell;
And both were as black as a witch's cat,
   And they loved each other well.

He had a tail, and she had a tail,
   Both long, and curling, and fine;
And each said: 'Yours is the finest tail
   In the world, excepting mine.'

He smelt the cheese, and she smelt the cheese,
   And they both pronounced it good;
And both said it would greatly add
   To the charms of their daily food.

So he went out, and she went out,
   And I saw them go with pain;
And what befell them I never can tell,
   For they never came back again.

Anon.

SONG OF THE SATYRS

Buzz, quoth the blue fly,
   Hum, quoth the bee,
Buzz and hum they cry,
   And so do we:
In his ear, in his nose,
   Thus do you see,
He ate the dormouse,
   Else it was thee.

Ben Jonson

SONG

The Owl is abroad,
The Bat and the Toad,
And so is the Cat-a-mountain;
The Ant and the Mole
Sit both in a hole,
And the Frog peeps out of the fountain.

Anon.

A DREAM

Once a dream did weave a shade
O'er my Angel-guarded bed,
That an emmet lost its way
Where on grass methought I lay.

Troubled, 'wilder'd, and forlorn,
Dark, benighted, travel-worn,
Over many a tangled spray,
All heart-broke I heard her say:

'O my children! do they cry?
Do they hear their father sigh?
Now they look abroad to see:
Now return and weep for me.'

Pitying, I dropp'd a tear;
But I saw a glow-worm near,
Who replied: 'What wailing wight
Calls the watchman of the night?

'I am set to light the ground,
While the beetle goes his round:
Follow now the beetle's hum;
Little wanderer, hie thee home.'

William Blake

A SONG

A widow bird sate mourning for her love
  Upon a wintry bough;
The frozen wind crept on above,
  The freezing stream below.

There was no leaf upon the forest bare,
  No flower upon the ground,
And little motion in the air
  Except the mill-wheel's sound.

Percy Bysshe Shelley

THE ZEBRAS

FROM the dark woods that breathe of fallen showers,
Harnessed with level rays in golden reins,
The zebras draw the dawn across the plains
Wading knee-deep among the scarlet flowers.
The sunlight, zithering their flanks with fire,
Flashes between the shadows as they pass
Barred with electric tremors through the grass
Like wind along the gold strings of a lyre.

Into the flushed air snorting rosy plumes
That smoulder round their feet in drifting fumes,
With dove-like voices call the distant fillies,
While round the herds the stallion wheels his flight,
Engine of beauty volted with delight,
To roll his mare among the trampled lilies.

Roy Campbell.

THE OWL

When cats run home and light is come,
  And dew is cold upon the ground,
And the far-off stream is dumb,
  And the whirring sail goes round,
  And the whirring sail goes round;
    Alone and warming his five wits,
    The white owl in the belfry sits.

When merry milkmaids click the latch,
  And rarely smells the new-mown hay,
And the cock hath sung beneath the thatch
  Twice or thrice his roundelay,
  Twice or thrice his roundelay;
    Alone and warming his five wits,
    The white owl in the belfry sits.

Alfred Tennyson

THE CUCKOO

The Cuckoo she's a pretty bird,
    She sings as she flies,
She brings us good tidings,
    She tells us no lies.

She suppeth white flowers
    For to keep her voice clear,
And the more she sings 'Cuckoo'
    The summer draws near.

O were I a scholar
    And could handle the pen,
I would write to my lover,
    And all falsehearted men.

I would bid them remember
    The bird as she flies,
I would bid them remember
    The flower as it dies.

Anon.

THE CORMORANT

The common cormorant or shag
Lays eggs inside a paper bag
The reason you will see no doubt
It is to keep the lightning out
But what these unobservant birds
Have never noticed is that herds
Of wandering bears may come with buns
And steal the bags to hold the crumbs.

Anon.

47

AN ELEGY ON THE DEATH OF
A MAD DOG

Good people all, of every sort,
    Give ear unto my song;
And if you find it wondrous short,
    It cannot hold you long.

In Islington there was a man,
    Of whom the world might say,
That still a godly race he ran,
    Whene'er he went to pray.

A kind and gentle heart he had,
    To comfort friends and foes;
The naked every day he clad,
    When he put on his clothes.

And in that town a dog was found,
    As many dogs there be,
Both mongrel, puppy, whelp, and hound,
    And curs of low degree.

This dog and man at first were friends;
    But when a pique began,
The dog, to gain some private ends,
    Went mad, and bit the man.

Around from all the neighbouring streets
    The wondering neighbours ran,
And swore the dog had lost his wits,
    To bite so good a man.

The wound it seemed both sore and sad
    To every Christian eye;
And while they swore the dog was mad,
    They swore the man would die.

But soon a wonder came to light,
   That showed the rogues they lied;
The man recovered of the bite,
   The dog it was that died.

Oliver Goldsmith

DUCKS' DITTY

All along the backwater,
Through the rushes tall,
Ducks are a-dabbling,
Up tails all!

Ducks' tails, drakes' tails,
Yellow feet a-quiver,
Yellow bills all out of sight
Busy in the river!

Slushy green undergrowth
Where the roach swim —
Here we keep our larder,
Cool and full and dim.

Every one for what he likes!
We like to be
Head down, tails up,
Dabbling free!

High in the blue above
Swifts whirl and call —
We are down a-dabbling
Up tails all!

Kenneth Grahame

49

THE SONG OF THE JELLICLES

Jellicle Cats come out to-night,
Jellicle Cats come one come all:
The Jellicle Moon is shining bright —
Jellicles come to the Jellicle Ball.

Jellicle Cats are black and white,
Jellicle Cats are rather small;
Jellicle Cats are merry and bright,
And pleasant to hear when they caterwaul.
Jellicle Cats have cheerful faces,
Jellicle Cats have bright black eyes;
They like to practise their airs and graces
And wait for the Jellicle Moon to rise.

Jellicle Cats develop slowly,
Jellicle Cats are not too big;
Jellicle Cats are roly-poly,
They know how to dance a gavotte and a jig.
Until the Jellicle Moon appears
They make their toilette and take their repose:
Jellicle wash behind their ears,
Jellicles dry between their toes.

Jellicle Cats are white and black,
Jellicle Cats are of moderate size;
Jellicles jump like a jumping-jack,
Jellicle Cats have moonlit eyes.
They're quiet enough in the morning hours,
They're quiet enough in the afternoon,
Reserving their terpsichorean powers
To dance by the light of the Jellicle Moon.

Jellicle Cats are black and white,
Jellicle Cats (as I said) are small;
If it happens to be a stormy night
They will practise a caper or two in the hall.
If it happens the sun is shining bright
You would say they had nothing to do at all:
They are resting and saving themselves to be right
For the Jellicle Moon and the Jellicle Ball.

T.S. Eliot

HEAVEN

Fish (fly-replete, in depth of June,
Dawdling away their wat'ry noon)
Ponder deep wisdom, dark or clear,
Each secret fishy hope or fear.
Fish say, they have their Stream and Pond;
But is there anything Beyond?
This life cannot be All, they swear,
For how unpleasant, if it were!
One may not doubt that, somehow, Good
Shall come of Water and of Mud;
And, sure, the reverent eye must see
A Purpose in Liquidity.
We darkly know, by Faith we cry,
The future is not Wholly Dry.
Mud unto mud! — Death eddies near —
Not here the appointed End, not here!
But somewhere, beyond Space and Time,
Is wetter water, slimier slime!
And there (they trust) there swimmeth One
Who swam ere rivers were begun,
Immense, of fishy form and mind,
Squamous, omnipotent, and kind;

51

And under that Almighty Fin,
The littlest fish may enter in.
Oh! never fly conceals a hook,
Fish say, in the Eternal Brook,
But more than mundane weeds are there,
And mud, celestially fair;
Fat caterpillars drift around,
And Paradisal grubs are found;
Unfading moths, immortal flies,
And the worm that never dies.
And in that Heaven of all their wish,
There shall be no more land, say fish.

Rupert Brooke

CIRCUS LION

Lumbering haunches, pussyfoot tread, a pride of
Lions under the arcs
Walk in, leap up, sit pedestalled there and glum
As a row of Dickensian clerks.

Their eyes are slag. Only a muscle flickering,
A bored, theatrical roar
Witness now to the furnaces that drove them
Exultant along the spoor.

In preyward, elastic leap they are sent through paper
Hoops at another's will
And a whip's crack: afterwards, in their cages,
They tear the provided kill.

Caught young, can this public animal ever dream of
Stars, distances and thunders?
Does he twitch in sleep for ticks, dried water-holes,
Rogue elephants, or hunters?

Sawdust, nor burning desert, is the ground
Of his to-fro, to-fro pacing,
Barred with the zebra shadows that imply
Sun's free wheel, man's coercing.

See this abdicated beast, once king
Of them all, nibble his claws:
Not anger enough left — no, nor despair —
To break his teeth on the bars.

C. Day Lewis

THE EAGLE

He clasps the crag with crooked hands;
Close to the sun in lonely lands,
Ring'd with the azure world, he stands.

The wrinkled sea beneath him crawls;
He watches from his mountain walls,
And like a thunderbolt he falls.

Alfred Tennyson

THE TIGER

Tiger! Tiger! burning bright
In the forests of the night,
What immortal hand or eye
Could frame thy fearful symmetry?

In what distant deeps or skies
Burnt the fire of thine eyes?
On what wings dare he aspire?
What the hand dare seize the fire?

And what shoulder and what art
Could twist the sinews of thy heart?
And when thy heart began to beat,
What dread hand? and what dread feet?

What the hammer? What the chain?
In what furnace was thy brain?
What the anvil? What dread grasp
Dare its deadly terrors clasp?

When the stars threw down their spears,
And water'd heaven with their tears,
Did he smile his work to see?
Did he who made the lamb make thee?

Tiger! Tiger burning bright
In the forests of the night,
What immortal hand or eye
Dare frame thy fearful symmetry?

William Blake

From A MIDSUMMER-NIGHT'S DREAM

Theseus: My hounds are bred out of the Spartan kind:
So flewed, so sanded; and their heads are hung
With ears that sweep away the morning dew —
Crook-kneed, and dewlapped like Thessalian bulls;
Slow in pursuit; but matched in mouth like bells,
Each under each. A cry more tuneable
Was never hollaed to, nor cheered with horn,
In crete, in Sparta, nor in Thessaly.

William Shakespeare

EPITAPH ON A HARE

Here lies, whom hound did ne'er pursue,
    Nor swifter greyhound follow,
Whose foot ne'er tainted morning dew,
    Nor ear heard huntsman's hallo',

Old Tiney, surliest of his kind,
    Who, nurs'd with tender care,
And to domestic bounds confin'd,
    Was still a wild Jack-hare.

Though duly from my hand he took
    His pittance ev'ry night,
He did it with a jealous look,
    And, when he could, would bite.

His diet was of wheaten bread,
    And milk, and oats, and straw,
Thistles, or lettuces instead,
    With sand to scour his maw.

On twigs of hawthorn he regal'd,
    On pippins' russet peel;
And when his juicy salads fail'd,
    Slic'd carrot pleas'd him well.

A Turkey carpet was his lawn,
    Whereon he lov'd to bound,
To skip and gambol like a fawn,
    And swing his rump around.

His frisking was at evening hours,
    For then he lost his fear;
But most before approaching show'rs,
    Or when a storm drew near.

Eight years and five round-rolling moons
  He thus saw steal away,
Dozing out all his idle noons,
  And ev'ry night at play.

I kept him for his humour's sake,
  For he would oft beguile
My heart of thoughts that made it ache,
  And force me to a smile.

But now, beneath this walnut shade
  He finds his long, last home,
And waits in snug concealment laid,
  'Till gentler Puss shall come.

He, still more aged, feels the shocks
  From which no care can save,
And, partner once of Tiney's box,
  Must soon partake his grave.

William Cowper

THE WHITE HARE

At the field's edge,
In the snow-furred sedge,
Couches the white hare;
Her stronghold is there.

Brown as the seeding grass
In summer she was,
With a creamed belly soft as ermine;
Beautiful she was among vermin.

Silky young she had,
For her spring was glad;
On the fell above
She ran races with love.
Softly she went
In and out of the tent
Of the tasselled corn;
Till the huntsman's horn
Raised the bogey death
And she was gone, like breath.

Thanks to her senses five
This charmer is alive:
Who cheated the loud pack,
Biting steel, poacher's sack;
Among the steep rocks
Outwitted the fanged fox.

And now winter has come;
Winds have made dumb
Water's crystal chime;
In a cloak of rime
Stands the stiff bracken;
Until the cold slacken
Beauty and terror kiss;
There is no armistice.
Low must the hare lie,
With great heart and round eye.

Wind-scoured and sky-burned
The fell was her feet spurned
In the flowery season
Of her swift unreason;
Gone is her March rover;
Now noon is soon over;

Now the dark falls
Heavily from sheer walls
Of snow-cumbering cloud,
And Earth shines in her shroud.
All things now fade
That were in love's image made.

She too must decrease
Unto a thorny peace,
Who put her faith
In this flesh, in this wraith.
A hoar habit borrows
Our light lady of sorrows,
Nor is her lot strange;
Time rings a snow-change.

Lilian Bowes Lyon

THE CORBIE AND THE CROW

The corbie with his roupie throat
Cried from the leafless tree,
'Come o'er the loch, come o'er the loch,
Come o'er the loch wi' me!'

The crow put out his sooty head,
And cried 'Where to, where to?'
'To yonder field', the corbie cried,
Where there is corn enoo.

'The ploughman ploughed the land yestreen,
The farmer sowed this morn,
And we can make a full fat meal,
From off the broad cast corn.'

The two black birds flew o'er the trees,
They flew towards the sun;
The farmer watching by the hedge
Shot both with his lang gun.

Anon.

THE GREATER CATS

The greater cats with golden eyes
Stare out between the bars.
Deserts are there, and different skies,
And night with different stars.
They prowl the aromatic hill,
And mate as fiercely as they kill,
And hold the freedom of their will
To roam, to live, to drink their fill;
But this beyond their wit know I:
Man lives a little, and for long shall die.

Their kind across the desert range
Where tulips spring from stones,
Not knowing they will suffer change
Or vultures pick their bones.
Their strength's eternal in their sight,
They rule the terror of the night,
They overtake the deer in flight,
And in their arrogance they smite;
But I am sage, if they are strong:
Man's love is transient as his death is long.

Yet oh what powers to deceive!
My wit is turned to faith,
And at this moment I believe
In love, and scout at death.
I came from nowhere, and shall be
Strong, steadfast, swift, eternally:
I am a lion, a stone, a tree,
And as the Polar star in me
Is fixed my constant heart on thee.
Ah, may I stay forever blind
With lions, tigers, leopards, and their kind.

V. Sackville-West

ON A FAVOURITE CAT

'Twas on a lofty vase's side,
Where China's gayest art had dyed
   The azure flowers that blow;
Demurest of the tabby kind,
The pensive Selima reclined,
   Gazed on the lake below.

Her conscious tail her joy declared;
The fair round face, the snowy beard,
   The velvet of her paws,
Her coat, that with the tortoise vies,
Her ears of jet, and emerald eyes,
   She saw; and purr'd applause.

Still had she gazed; but midst the tide
Two angel forms were seen to glide,
   The Genii of the stream:
Their scaly armour's Tyrian hue
Thro' richest purple to the view
   Betray'd a golden gleam.

The hapless Nymph with wonder saw:
A whisker first and then a claw,
   With many an ardent wish,
She stretch'd in vain to reach the prize,
What female heart can gold despise?
   What Cat's averse to fish?

Presumptuous Maid! with looks intent
Again she stretch'd, again she bent,
   Nor knew the gulf between.
(Malignant Fate sat by, and smiled)
The slipp'ry verge her feet beguiled,
   She tumbled headlong in.

Eight times emerging from the flood
She mew'd to ev'ry wat'ry god,
    Some speedy aid to send.
No Dolphin came, no Nereid stirr'd:
Nor cruel *Tom*, nor *Susan* heard,
    A Fav'rite has no friend!

From hence, ye Beauties, undeceived,
Know, one false step is ne'er retrieved,
    And be with caution bold.
Not all that tempts your wand'ring eyes
And heedless hearts, is lawful prize;
    Nor all that glisters, gold.

                                   Thomas Gray

SEDGE—WARBLERS

This beauty made me dream there was a time
Long past and irrecoverable, a clime
Where any brook so radiant racing clear
Through buttercup and kingcup bright as brass
But gentle, nourishing the meadow grass
That leans and scurries in the wind, would bear
Another beauty, divine and feminine,
Child to the sun, a nymph whose soul unstained
Could love all day, and never hate or tire,
A lover of mortal or immortal kin.

And yet, rid of this dream, ere I had drained
Its poison, quieted was my desire
So that I only looked into the water,
Clearer than any goddess or man's daughter,

And hearkened while it combed the dark green hair
And shook the millions of the blossoms white
Of water-crowfoot, and curdled to one sheet
The flowers fallen from the chestnuts in the park
Far off. And sedge-warblers, clinging so light
To willow twigs, sang longer than the lark,
Quick, shrill, or grating, a song to match the heat
Of the strong sun, nor less the water's cool,
Gushing through narrows, swirling in the pool.
Their song that lacks all words, all melody,
All sweetness almost, was dearer then to me
Than sweetest voice that sings in tune sweet words.
This was the best of May — the small brown birds
Wisely reiterating endlessly
What no man learnt yet, in or out of school.

Edward Thomas

THE FLEA

Mark but this flea, and mark in this,
How little that which thou deny'st me is;
It suck'd me first, and now sucks thee,
And in this flea, our two bloods mingled be;
Thou know'st that this cannot be said
A sin, nor shame, nor loss of maidenhead,
   Yet this enjoys before it woo,
    And pamper'd swells with one blood made of two,
   And this, alas, is more than we would do.

Oh stay, three lives in one flea spare,
Where we almost, yea more than married are.
This flea is you and I, and this
Our marriage bed, and marriage temple is;
Though parents grudge, and you, we're met,
And cloistered in these living walls of jet.

Though use make you apt to kill me,
Let not to that, self murder added be,
And sacrilege, three sins in killing three.

Cruel and sudden, hast thou since
Purpled thy nail, in blood of innocence?
Wherein could this flea guilty be,
Except in that drop which it suck'd from thee?
Yet thou triumph'st, and say'st that thou
Find'st not thyself, nor me the weaker now;
   'Tis true, then learn how false, fears be;
   Just so much honour, when thou yield'st to me,
   Will waste, as this flea's death took life from thee.

John Donne

THE MOSQUITO

When did you start your tricks,
Monsieur?

What do you stand on such high legs for?
Why this length of shredded shank,
You exaltation?

Is it so that you shall lift your centre of gravity upwards
And weigh no more than air as you alight upon me,
Stand upon me weightless, you phantom?

I heard a woman call you the Winged Victory
In sluggish Venice.
You turn your head towards your tail, and smile.

How can you put so much devilry
Into that translucent phantom shred
Of a frail corpus?

Queer, with your thin wings and your streaming legs,
How you sail like a heron, or a dull clot of air,
A nothingness.

Yet what an aura surrounds you;
Your evil little aura, prowling, and casting a numbness on
    my mind.

That is your trick, your bit of filthy magic:
Invisibility, and the anaesthetic power
To deaden my attention in your direction.

But I know your game now, streaky sorcerer.
Queer, how you stalk and prowl the air
In circles and evasions, enveloping me,
Ghoul on wings
Winged Victory.

Settle, and stand on long thin shanks
Eyeing me sideways, and cunningly conscious that I am aware,
You speck.

I hate the way you lurch off sideways into air
Having read my thoughts against you.

Come then, let us play at unawares,
And see who wins in this sly game of bluff.
Man or mosquito.

You don't know that I exist, and I don't know that you exist.
Now then!

It is your trump,
It is your hateful little trump,
You pointed fiend,

Which shakes my sudden blood to hatred of you:
It is your small, high, hateful bugle in my ear.

Why do you do it?
Surely it is bad policy.

They say you can't help it.

If that is so, then I believe a little in Providence
   protecting the innocent.
But it sounds so amazingly like a slogan,
A yell of triumph as you snatch my scalp.

Blood, red blood
Super-magical
Forbidden liquor.

I behold you stand
For a second enspasmed in oblivion,
Obscenely ecstasied
Sucking live blood,
My blood.

Such silence, such suspended transport,
Such gorging,
Such obscenity of trespass.

You stagger
As well as you may.
Only your accursed hairy frailty,
Your own imponderable weightlessness
Saves you, wafts you away on the very draught my
   anger makes in its snatching.

Away with a paean of derision,
You winged blood-drop.

Can I not overtake you?
Are you one too many for me,
Winged Victory?
Am I not mosquito enough to out-mosquito you?

Queer, what a big stain my sucked blood makes
Beside the infinitesimal faint smear of you!
Queer, what a dim dark smudge you have disappeared
    into!

D.H. Lawrence

THE WINDHOVER
To Christ Our Lord

I caught this morning morning's minion, king-
    dom of daylight's dauphin, dapple-dawn-drawn Fal-
        con, in his riding
    Of the rolling level underneath him steady air, and
        striding
High there, how he rung upon the rein of a wimpling wing
In his ecstasy! then off, off forth on swing,
    As a skate's heel sweeps smooth on a bow-bend: the
        hurl and gliding
    Rebuffed the big wind. My heart in hiding
Stirred for a bird, — the achieve of, the mastery of the
        thing!

Brute beauty and valour and act, oh, air, pride, plume, here
    Buckle! AND the fire that breaks from thee then, a
        billion
Times told lovelier, more dangerous, O my chevalier!

No wonder of it: sheer plòd makes plough down
    sillion
Shine, and blue-bleak embers, ah my dear,
    Fall, gall themselves, and gash gold-vermilion.

Gerard Manley Hopkins

From IN MEMORIAM

Unwatch'd, the garden bough shall sway,
    The tender blossom flutter down,
    Unloved, that beech will gather brown,
This maple burn itself away;

Unloved, the sun-flower, shining fair,
    Ray round with flames her disk of seed,
    And many a rose-carnation feed
With summer spice the humming air;

Unloved, by many a sandy bar,
    The brook shall babble down the plain,
    At noon or when the lesser wain
Is twisting round the polar star;

Uncared for, gird the windy grove,
    And flood the haunts of hern and crake;
    Or into silver arrows break
The sailing moon in creek and cove;

Till from the garden and the wild
    A fresh association blow,
    And year by year the landscape grow
Familiar to the stranger's child;

As year by year the labourer tills
    His wonted glebe, or lops the glades;
    And year by year our memory fades
From all the circle of the hills.

Alfred Tennyson

From THE GARDEN AT APPLETON HOUSE

See how the flowers as at parade,
Under the colours stand displayed;
Each regiment in order grows,
That of the tulip, pink, and rose.
But when the vigilant patrol
Of stars walks round about the pole,
Their leaves that to the stalks are curled
Seem to their staves the ensigns furled.
Then in some flower's belovèd hut,
Each bee, as sentinel, is shut,
And sleeps so too, but, if once stirred,
She runs you through, nor asks the word.
   O thou, that dear and happy isle,
The garden of the world erewhile,
Thou Paradise of the four seas,
Which Heaven planted us to please,
But, to exclude the world, did guard
With watery, if not flaming sword, –
What luckless apple did we taste
To make us mortal and thee waste?
Unhappy! shall we never more
That sweet militia restore,
When gardens only had their towers
And all the garrisons were flowers;
When roses only arms might bear,
And men did rosy garlands wear?

Andrew Marvell

From THE WINTER'S TALE

I would I had some flowers o'th' spring that might
Become your time of day; and yours and yours,
That wear upon your virgin branches yet
Your maidenheads growing: O Proserpina,
For the flowers now, that frighted thou let'st fall
From Dis's waggon! daffodils,

68

That come before the swallow dares, and take
The winds of March with beauty; violets (dim,
But sweeter than the lids of Juno's eyes
Or Cytherea's breath); pale primroses,
That die unmarried, ere they can behold
Bright Phoebus in his strength (a malady
Most incident to maids); bold oxlips and
The crown imperial; lilies of all kinds,
The flower-de-luce being one! O, these I lack,
To make you garlands of —

William Shakespeare

THE QUESTION

I dreamed that, as I wandered by the way,
   Bare winter suddenly was changed to spring,
And gentle odours led my steps astray,
   Mixed with a sound of waters murmuring
Along a shelving bank of turf, which lay
   Under a copse, and hardly dared to fling

Its green arms round the bosom of the stream,
But kissed it and then fled, as thou mightest in dream.

There grew pied wind-flowers and violets,
   Daisies, those pearled Arcturi of the earth,
The constellated flower that never sets;
   Faint oxlips; tender bluebells, at whose birth
The sod scarce heaved; and that tall flower that wets —
   Like a child, half in tenderness and mirth —
Its mother's face with heaven's collected tears,
When the low wind, its playmate's voice, it hears.

And in the warm hedge grew lush eglantine,
   Green cow-bind and the moonlight-coloured May,
And cherry-blossoms, and white cups, whose wine
   Was the bright dew, yet drained not by the day;
And wild roses, and ivy serpentine,
With its dark buds and leaves, wandering astray;
And flowers azure, black, and streaked with gold,
Fairer than any wakened eyes behold.

And nearer to the river's trembling edge
   There grew broad flag-flowers, purple prankt with white,
And starry river buds among the sedge,
   And floating water-lilies, broad and bright,
Which lit the oak that overhung the hedge
   With moonlight beams of their own watery light;
And bulrushes, and reeds of such deep green
As soothed the dazzled eye with sober sheen.

Methought that of these visionary flowers
   I made a nosegay, bound in such a way
That the same hues, which in their natural bowers
   Were mingled or opposed, the like array
Kept these imprisoned children of the Hours
   Within my hand — and then, elate and gay,
I hastened to the spot whence I had come,
That I might there present it! — Oh! to whom?

Percy Bysshe Shelley

4
LOVE AND FRIENDSHIP

...Love is not love
Which alters when it alteration finds

SHAKESPEARE

LOVE AND AGE

I play'd with you 'mid cowslips blowing,
   When I was six and you were four;
When garlands weaving, flower-balls throwing,
   Were pleasures soon to please no more.
Through groves and meads, o'er grass and heather,
   With little playmates, to and fro,
We wander'd hand in hand together;
   But that was sixty years ago.

You grew a lovely roseate maiden,
   And still our early love was strong;
Still with no care our days were laden,
   They glided joyously along;
And I did love you very dearly,
   How dearly words want power to show;
I thought your heart was touch'd as nearly;
   But that was fifty years ago.

Then other lovers came around you,
   Your beauty grew from year to year,
And many a splendid circle found you
   The centre of its glittering sphere.
I saw you then, first vows forsaking,
   On rank and wealth your hand bestow;
O, then I thought my heart was breaking! –
   But that was forty years ago.

And I lived on, to wed another:
   No cause she gave me to repine;
And when I heard you were a mother,
   I did not wish the children mine.
My own young flock, in fair progression,
   Made up a pleasant Christmas row:
My joy in them was past expression;
   But that was thirty years ago.

You grew a matron plump and comely,
    You dwelt in fashion's brightest blaze;
My earthly lot was far more homely;
    But I too had my festal days.
No merrier eyes have ever glisten'd
    Around the hearth-stone's wintry glow,
Than when my youngest child was christen'd;
    But that was twenty years ago.

Time pass'd. My eldest girl was married,
    And I am now a grandsire gray;
One pet of four years old I've carried
    Among the wild-flower'd meads to play.
In our old fields of childish pleasure,
    Where now, as then, the cowslips blow,
She fills her basket's ample measure;
    And that is not ten years ago.

But though first love's impassion'd blindness
    Has pass'd away in colder light,
I still have thought of you with kindness,
    And shall do, till our last good-night.
The ever-rolling silent hours
    Will bring a time we shall not know,
When our young days of gathering flowers
    Will be an hundred years ago.

                    Thomas Love Peacock

CHLOE'S A NYMPH

Chloe's a Nymph in flowery groves,
    A Nereid in the streams;
Saint-like she in the temple moves,
    A woman in my dreams.

Love steals artillery from her eyes,
　The Graces point her charms;
Orpheus is rivall'd in her voice,
　And Venus in her arms.

Never so happily in one
　Did heaven and earth combine:
And yet 'tis flesh and blood alone
　That makes her so divine.

Thomas D'Urfey

THE TRIUMPH OF CHARIS

See the Chariot at hand here of Love,
　Wherein my Lady rideth!
Each that draws is a swan or a dove,
　And well the car Love guideth.
As she goes, all hearts do duty
　　　　Unto her beauty;
And enamoured do wish, so they might
　　　　But enjoy such a sight,
That they still were to run by her side,
Thorough swards, thorough seas, whither she would ride.

Do but look on her eyes, they do light
    All that Love's world compriseth!
Do but look on her hair, it is bright
    As Love's star when it riseth!
Do but mark, her forehead's smoother
                Than words that soothe her;
And from her arched brows such a grace
                Sheds itself through the face,
As alone there triumphs to the life
All the gain, all the good, of the elements' strife.

Have you seen but a bright lily grow
    Before rude hands have touch'd it?
Have you mark'd but the fall of the snow
    Before the soil hath smutch'd it?
Have you felt the wool of beaver,
                Or swan's down ever?
Or have smelt o' the bud o' the brier,
                Or the nard in the fire?
Or have tasted the bag of the bee?
O so white, O so soft, O so sweet is she!

Ben Jonson

THE CROWNED HEART

Thou sent'st to me a heart was crowned;
    I took it to be thine,
But when I saw it had a wound
    I knew that heart was mine.
A bounty of a strange conceit!
    To send mine own to me,
And send it in a worse estate
    Than when it came to thee.

Anon.

I'LL NEVER LOVE THEE MORE

My dear and only Love, I pray
   That little world of thee
Be govern'd by no other sway
   Than purest monarchy;
For if confusion have a part
   (Which virtuous souls abhor),
And hold a synod in thine heart,
   I'll never love thee more.

Like Alexander I will reign,
   And I will reign alone;
My thoughts did evermore disdain
   A rival on my throne.
He either fears his fate too much,
   Or his deserts are small,
That dares not put it to the touch,
   To gain or lose it all.

And in the empire of thine heart,
   Where I should solely be,
If others do pretend a part
   Or dare to vie with me,
Or if *Committees* thou erect,
   And go on such a score,
I'll laugh and sing at thy neglect,
   And never love thee more.

But if thou wilt prove faithful then,
   And constant of thy word,
I'll make thee glorious by my pen
   And famous by my sword;
I'll serve thee in such noble ways
   Was never heard before;
I'll crown and deck thee all with bays,
   And love thee more and more.

The Marquis of Montrose

'MY TRUE LOVE HATH MY HEART'

My true love hath my heart, and I have his,
By just exchange one for another given:
I hold his dear, and mine he cannot miss,
There never was a better bargain driven:
My true love hath my heart, and I have his.

His heart in me keeps him and me in one,
My heart in him his thoughts and senses guides:
He loves my heart, for once it was his own,
I cherish his because in me it bides:
My true love hath my heart, and I have his.

Sir Philip Sidney

'NEVER SEEK TO TELL THY LOVE'

Never seek to tell thy love,
Love that never told can be;
For the gentle wind does move
Silently, invisibly.

I told my love, I told my love,
I told her all my heart;
Trembling, cold, in ghastly fears,
Ah! she doth depart.

Soon as she was gone from me,
A traveller came by,
Silently, invisibly:
He took her with a sigh.

William Blake

ANNIE LAURIE

Maxwelton braes are bonnie,
  Where early falls the dew,
And 'twas there that Annie Laurie
  Gied me her promise true;
Gied me her promise true,
  Which ne'er forgot shall be,
And for bonnie Annie Laurie,
  I'd lay me doon and dee.

Her brow is like the snow-flake,
  Her neck is like the swan,
Her face it is the fairest
  That e'er the sun shone on;
That e'er the sun shone on,
  And dark blue is her e'e;
And for bonnie Annie Laurie
  I'd lay me doon and dee.

Like dew on the gowans lying,
  Is the fall of her fairy feet;
And like winds in summer sighing,
  Her voice is low and sweet;
Her voice is low and sweet,
  And she's a' the world to me;
And for bonnie Annie Laurie
  I'd lay me doon and dee.

           Anon.

UPON A DELAYING LADY

Come, come away,
Or let me go;
Must I here stay
Because y'are slow,
And will continue so?
Troth lady, no

I scorn to be
A slave to state:
And since I'm free,
I will not wait,
Henceforth at such a rate,
For needy fate.

If you desire
My spark should glow,
The peeping fire
You must blow,
Or I shall quickly grow
To Frost or Snow.

Robert Herrick

From 'THE MAGNETIC MOUNTAIN'

Live you by love confined,
There is no nearer nearness;
Break not his light bounds,
The stars' and seas' harness:
There is nothing beyond,
We have found the land's end.
We'll take no mortal wound
Who felt him in the furnace,
Drowned in his fierceness,
By his midsummer browned:
Nor ever lose awareness
Of nearness and farness
Who've stood at earth's heart careless
Of suns and storms around,
Who have leant on the hedge of the wind,
On the last ledge of darkness.

We are where love has come
To live: he is that river
Which flows and is the same;
He is not the famous deceiver
Nor early-flowering dream.
Content you. Be at home
In me. There's but one room
Of all the house you may never
Share, deny or enter.
There, as a candle's beam
Stands firm and will not waver
Spire-straight in a close chamber,
As though in shadowy cave a
Stalagmite of flame,
The integral spirit climbs
The dark in light for ever.

C. Day Lewis

'SO WE'LL GO NO MORE A-ROVING'

So, we'll go no more a-roving
    So late into the night,
Though the heart be still as loving,
    And the moon be still as bright.

For the sword outwears its sheath,
    And the soul wears out the breast,
And the heart must pause to breathe,
    And love itself have rest.

Though the night was made for loving,
    And the day returns too soon,
Yet we'll go no more a-roving
    By the light of the moon.

Lord Byron

SONG

Ask me no more where Jove bestows,
When June is past, the fading rose:
For in your beauty's orient deep
These flowers, as in their causes, sleep.

Ask me no more whither do stray
The golden atoms of the day:
For in pure love Heaven did prepare
Those powders to enrich your hair.

Ask me no more whither doth haste
The nightingale when May is past:
For in your sweet dividing throat
She winters and keeps warm her note.

Ask me no more where those stars light
That downwards fall in dead of night:
For in your eyes they sit, and there
Fixèd become as in their sphere.

Ask me no more if east or west
The Phoenix builds her spicy nest:
For unto you at last she flies,
And in your fragrant bosom dies.

Thomas Carew

UPON JULIA'S CLOTHES

When as in silks my Julia goes,
Then, then, methinks, how sweetly flows
That liquefaction of her clothes.

Next, when I cast mine eyes and see
That brave Vibration each way free;
O how that glittering taketh me!

Robert Herrick

THE SUN RISING

Busy old fool, unruly Sun,
   Why dost thou thus,
Through windows, and through curtains call on us?
Must to thy motions lovers' seasons run?
    Saucy, pedantic wretch, go chide
    Late school boys, and sour prentices,
  Go tell Court-huntsmen, that the King will ride,
  Call country ants to harvest offices;
Love, all alike, no season knows, nor clime,
Nor hours, days, months, which are the rags of time.

    Thy beams, so reverend, and strong
    Why shouldst thou think?
I could eclipse and cloud them with a wink,
But that I would not lose her sight so long:
    If her eyes have not blinded thine,
    Look, and to-morrow late, tell me,
  Whether both the' India's of spice and mine
  Be where thou left'st them, or lie here with me.
Ask for those Kings whom thou saw'st yesterday,
And thou shalt hear, All here in one bed lay.

    She'is all States, and all Princes, I,
    Nothing else is.
Princes do but play us; compar'd to this,
All honour's mimic; All wealth alchemy.
    Thou sun art half as happy as we,
    In that the world's contracted thus;
  Thine age asks ease, and since thy duties be
  To warm the world, that's done in warming us.
Shine here to us, and thou art everywhere;
This bed thy centre is, these walls, thy sphere.

John Donne

SONG FROM 'THE SILENT WOMAN'

Still to be neat, still to be drest,
As you were going to a feast;
Still to be powder'd, still perfumed:
Lady, it is to be presumed,
Though art's hid causes are not found,
All is not sweet, all is not sound.

Give me a look, give me a face
That makes simplicity a grace;
Robes loosely flowing, hair as free:
Such sweet neglect more taketh me
Than all th' adulteries of art;
They strike mine eyes, but not my heart.

Ben Jonson

ON A CERTAIN LADY AT COURT

I know a thing that's most uncommon;
　(Envy, be silent and attend!)
I know a reasonable woman,
　Handsome and witty, yet a friend.

Not warp'd by passion, awed by rumour;
　Not grave through pride, nor gay through folly;
An equal mixture of good-humour
　And sensible soft melancholy.

'Has she no faults then (Envy says), Sir?'
　Yes, she has one, I must aver:
When all the world conspires to praise her,
　The woman's deaf, and does not hear.

Alexander Pope

TO ALTHEA FROM PRISON

When Love with unconfinèd wings
   Hovers within my gates,
And my divine Althea brings
   To whisper at the grates;
When I lie tangled in her hair,
   And fetter'd to her eye;
The birds, that wanton in the air
   Know no such liberty.

When flowing cups run swiftly round
   With no allaying Thames,
Our careless heads with roses bound,
   Our hearts with loyal flames;
When thirsty grief in wine we steep,
   When healths and draughts go free,
Fishes that tipple in the deep
   Know no such liberty.

When, like committed linnets, I
   With shriller throat shall sing
The sweetness, mercy, majesty,
   And glories of my King;
When I shall voice aloud, how good
   He is, how Great should be
Enlarged winds, that curl the flood,
   Know no such liberty.

Stone walls do not a prison make,
   Nor iron bars a cage;
Minds innocent and quiet take
   That for an hermitage;
If I have freedom in my love,
   And in my soul am free,
Angels alone, that soar above,
   Enjoy such liberty.

                 Richard Lovelace

'HE THAT LOVES A ROSY CHEEK'

He that loves a rosy cheek,
  Or a coral lip admires,
Or from star-like eyes doth seek
  Fuel to maintain his fires:
As old Time makes these decay,
So his flames must waste away.

But a smooth and steadfast mind,
  Gentle thoughts and calm desires,
Hearts with equal love combined,
  Kindle never-dying fires.
Where these are not, I despise
Lovely cheeks or lips or eyes.

                          Thomas Carew

A PEDLAR

Fine knacks for ladies! cheap, choice, brave, and new,
  Good pennyworths — but money cannot move:
I keep a fair but for the Fair to view —
  A beggar may be liberal of love.
Though all my wares be trash, the heart is true.
                The heart is true.

Great gifts are guiles and look for gifts again;
  My trifles come as treasures from my mind:
It is a precious jewel to be plain;
  Sometimes in shell the orient'st pearls we find:-
Of others take a sheaf, of me a grain!
                Of me a grain!

                          Anon.

AS YE CAME FROM THE HOLY LAND

As ye came from the holy land
    Of Walsinghame,
Met you not with my true love
    By the way as you came?

How should I know your true love,
    That have met many a one
As I came from the holy land,
    That have come, that have gone?

She is neither white nor brown
    But as the heavens fair;
There is none hath her form divine
    In the earth or the air.

Such a one did I meet, good sir,
    Such an angelic face,
Who like a nymph, like a queen, did appear
    In her gait, in her grace.

She hath left me here alone
    All alone, as unknown,
Who sometime did me lead with herself,
    And me loved as her own.

What's the cause that she leaves you alone
    And a new way doth take,
That sometime did love you as her own,
    And her joy did you make?

I have loved her all my youth,
    But now am old, as you see:
Love likes not the falling fruit,
    Nor the withered tree.

Know that Love is a careless child,
    And forgets promise past:

He is blind, he is deaf when he list,
    And in faith never fast.

His desire is a dureless content,
    And a trustless joy;
He is won with a world of despair,
    And is lost with a toy.

Of womenkind such indeed is the love,
    Or the word love abusèd,
Under which many childish desires
    And conceits are excusèd.

But true love is a durable fire,
    In the mind ever burning,
Never sick, never dead, never cold,
    From itself never turning.

*Anon. (doubtfully attributed
to Sir Walter Raleigh)*

THE GOOD-MORROW

I wonder by my troth, what thou and I
Did, till we lov'd? were we not wean'd till then?
But suck'd on country pleasures, childishly?
Or snorted we in the seven sleepers' den?
'Twas so; but this, all pleasures fancies be.
If ever any beauty I did see,
Which I desir'd, and got, 'twas but a dream of thee.

And now good-morrow to our waking souls,
Which watch not one another out of fear;
For love, all love of other sights controls,
And makes one little room an everywhere.

Let sea-discoverers to new worlds have gone,
Let maps to other, worlds on worlds have shown,
Let us possess one world, each hath one, and is one.

My face in thine eye, thine in mine appears,
And true plain hearts do in the faces rest;
Where can we find two better hemispheres
Without sharp North, without declining West?
What ever dies, was not mixt equally;
If our two loves be one, or, thou and I
Love so alike, that none do slacken, none can die.

John Donne

SONG

Follow thy fair sun, unhappy shadow!
   Though thou be black as night,
   And she made all of light,
Yet follow thy fair sun, unhappy shadow!

Follow her, whose light thy light depriveth!
   Though here thou liv'st disgraced,
   And she in heaven is placed,
Yet follow her whose light the world reviveth!

Follow those pure beams, whose beauty burneth!
   That so have scorchèd thee
   As thou still black must be,
Till her kind beams thy black to brightness turneth.

Follow her, while yet her glory shineth!
   There comes a luckless night
   That will dim all her light;
And this the black unhappy shade divineth.

Follow still, since so thy fates ordainèd!
   The sun must have his shade,
   Till both at once do fade, —
The sun still proud, the shadow still disdainèd.

Thomas Campion

WEDDED

They leave their love-lorn haunts,
Their sigh-warm floating Eden;
And they are mute at once,
Mortals by God unheeden,
By their past kisses chidden.

But they have kist and known
Clear things we dim by guesses —
Spirit to spirit grown:
Heaven, born in hand-caresses.
Love, fall from sheltering tresses.

And they are dumb and strange:
Bared trees bowed from each other,
Their last green interchange
What lost dreams shall discover?
Dead, strayed, to love-strange lover.

Isaac Rosenberg

'SINCE THERE'S NO HELP'

Since there's no help, come let us kiss and part —
Nay, I have done, you get no more of me;
And I am glad, yea, glad with all my heart,
That thus so cleanly I myself can free.
Shake hands for ever, cancel all our vows,
And when we meet at any time again,
Be it not seen in either of our brows,
That we one jot of former love retain.
Now at the last gasp of Love's latest breath,
When, his pulse failing, Passion speechless lies,
When Faith is kneeling by his bed of death,
And Innocence is closing up his eyes.
    — Now if thou woulds't, when all have given him over,
From death to life thou might'st him yet recover.

Michael Drayton

THE LOST MISTRESS

All's over, then: does truth sound bitter
    As one at first believes?
Hark, 'tis the sparrows' good-night twitter
    About your cottage eaves!

And the leaf-buds on the vine are woolly,
    I noticed that, today;
One day more bursts them open fully
    — You know the red turns grey.

To-morrow we meet the same then, dearest?
    May I take your hand in mine?
Mere friends are we, — well, friends the merest
    Keep much that I'll resign:

For each glance of that eye so bright and black,
    Though I keep with heart's endeavour, —
Your voice, when you wish the snowdrops back,
    Though it stay in my soul for ever! —

Yet I will but say what mere friends say,
    Or only a thought stronger;
I will hold your hand but as long as all may,
    Or so very little longer!

Robert Browning

SONG

Shall I, wasting in despair,
Die because a woman's fair?
Or make pale my cheeks with care
'Cause another's rosy are?
Be she fairer than the day,
Or the flow'ry meads in May,
    If she think not well of me,
    What care I how fair she be?

Shall my silly heart be pined
'Cause I see a woman kind?
Or a well disposèd nature
Joinèd with a lovely feature?
Be she meeker, kinder, than
Turtle-dover or pelican,
    If she be not so to me,
    What care I how kind she be?

Shall a woman's virtues move
Me to perish for her love?
Or her well-deservings known
Make me quite forget my own?
Be she with that goodness blest
Which may merit name of Best,
    If she be not such to me,
    What care I how good she be?

'Cause her fortune seems too high,
Shall I play the fool and die?
She that bears a noble mind,
If not outward helps she find,
Thinks what with them he would do
That without them dares her woo;
    And unless that mind I see,
    What care I how great she be?

Great, or good, or kind, or fair,
I will ne'er the more despair;
If she love me, this believe,
I will die ere she shall grieve;
If she slight me when I woo,
I can scorn and let her go;
    For if she be not for me,
    What care I for whom she be?

George Wither

91

THE FAIR SINGER

To make a final conquest of all me,
Love did compose so sweet an enemy,
In whom both beauties to my death agree,
Joining themselves in fatal harmony,
That, while she with her eyes my heart does bind,
She with her voice might captivate my mind.

I could have fled from one but singly fair;
My disentangled soul itself might save,
Breaking the curlèd trammels of her hair;
But how should I avoid to be her slave,
Whose subtle art invisibly can wreathe
My fetters of the very air I breathe?

It had been easy fighting in some plain,
Where victory might hang in equal choice,
But all resistance against her is vain,
Who has the advantage both of eyes and voice,
And all my forces needs must be undone,
She having gainèd both the wind and sun.

Andrew Marvell

SONG

When thou must home to shades of underground,
And there arrived, a new admirèd guest,
The beauteous spirits do engirt thee round,
White Iope, blithe Helen, and the rest,
To hear the stories of thy finish'd love
From that smooth tongue whose music hell can move;

Then wilt thou speak of banqueting delights,
Of masques and revels which sweet youth did make,
Of tourneys and great challenges of knights,
And all these triumphs for thy beauty's sake:
When thou hast told these honours done to thee,
Then tell, O tell, how thou didst murder me!

Thomas Campion

REMEMBRANCE

They flee from me that sometime did me seek,
 With naked foot stalking within my chamber:
Once have I seen them gentle, tame, and meek,
 That now are wild, and do not once remember
 That sometime they have put themselves in danger
To take bread at my hand; and now they range,
Busily seeking in continual change.

Thanked be fortune, it hath been otherwise
 Twenty times better; but once especial —
In thin array: after a pleasant guise,
 When her loose gown did from her shoulders fall,
 And she me caught in her arms long and small,
And therewithal so sweetly did me kiss,
And softly said, '*Dear heart, how like you this?*'

It was no dream; for I lay broad awaking:
 But all is turn'd now, through my gentleness,
Into a bitter fashion of forsaking;
 And I have leave to go of her goodness;
 And she also to use new-fangleness.
But since that I unkindly so am servèd,
'*How like you this?*' — what hath she now deservèd?

        Sir Thomas Wyatt

EARL MERTOUN'S SONG

There's a woman like a dew-drop, she's so purer than the
 purest;
And her noble heart's the noblest, yes, and her sure faith's
 the surest:
And her eyes are dark and humid, like the depth on depth
 of lustre
Hid i' the harebell, while her tresses, sunnier than the wild-
 grape cluster,

Gush in golden-tinted plenty down her neck's rose-misted
  marble:
Then her voice's music . . . call it the well's bubbling, the
  bird's warble!

And this woman says, 'My days were sunless and my nights
  were moonless,
Parch'd the pleasant April herbage, and the lark's hearts
  outbreak tuneless
If you loved me not!' And I who (ah, for words of flame!)
  adore her,
Who am mad to lay my spirit prostrate palpably before her —
I may enter at her portal soon, as now her lattice takes me,
And by noontide as by midnight make her mine, as hers she
  makes me!

Robert Browning

O FOR SOME
HONEST LOVER'S GHOST

O for some honest lover's ghost,
  Some kind unbodied post
    Sent from the shades below!
    I strangely long to know
Whether the nobler chaplets wear
Those that their mistress' scorn did bear
    Or those that were used kindly.

For whatso'er they tell us here
  To make those sufferings dear,
    'Twill there, I fear, be found
    That to the being crown'd
T' have loved alone will not suffice,
Unless we also have been wise
    And have our loves enjoy'd.

What posture can we think him in
  That, here unloved, again
    Departs, and's thither gone
    Where each sits by his own?
Or how can that Elysium be
Where I my mistress still must see
    Circled in other's arms?

For there the judges all are just,
  And Sophonisba must
    Be his whom she held dear,
    Not his who loved her here.
The sweet Philoclea, since she died,
Lies by her Pirocles his side,
    Not by Amphialus.

Some bays, perchance, or myrtle bough
  For difference crowns the brow
    Of those kind souls that were
    The noble martyrs here:
And if that be the only odds
(As who can tell?), ye kinder gods,
    Give me the woman here!

Sir John Suckling

THE ANNIVERSARY

All Kings, and all their favourites,
   All glory of honours, beauties, wits,
The Sun itself, which makes times, as they pass,
Is elder by a year, now, than it was
When thou and I first one another saw:
All other things to their destruction draw,
   Only our love hath no decay;
This, no to-morrow hath, nor yesterday,
Running it never runs from us away,
But truly keeps his first, last, everlasting day.

   Two graves must hide thine and my corse,
   If one might, death were no divorce.
Alas, as well as other Princes, we,
(Who Prince enough in one another be,)
Must leave at last in death, these eyes, and ears,
Oft fed with true oaths, and with sweet salt tears;
   But souls where nothing dwells but love
(All other thoughts being inmates) then shall prove
This, or a love increasèd there above,
When bodies to their graves, souls from their graves remove.

   And then we shall be throughly blest,
   But we no more, than all the rest;
Here upon earth, we're Kings, and none but we
Can be such Kings, nor of such subjects be.
Who is so safe as we? where none can do
Treason to us, except one of us two.
   True and false fears let us refrain,
Let us love nobly, and live, and add again
Years and years unto years, till we attain
To write threescore: this is the second of our reign.

John Donne

'MY MISTRESS' EYES'

My mistress' eyes are nothing like the sun,
Coral is far more red, than her lips red,
If snow be white, why then her breasts are dun:
If hairs be wires, black wires grow on her head:
I have seen roses damasked, red and white,
But no such roses see I in her cheeks,
And in some perfumes is there more delight,
Than in the breath that from my mistress reeks.
I love to hear her speak, yet well I know,
That music hath a far more pleasing sound:
I grant I never saw a goddess go,
My mistress when she walks treads on the ground.
    And yet by heaven I think my love as rare,
    As any she belied with false compare.

William Shakespeare

TO HIS COY MISTRESS

Had we but world enough, and time,
This coyness, lady, were no crime.
We would sit down, and think which way
To walk, and pass our long love's day.
Thou by the Indian Ganges' side
Shouldst rubies find: I by the tide
Of Humber would complain. I would
Love you ten years before the flood,
And you should, if you please, refuse
Till the conversion of the Jews;
My vegetable love should grow
Vaster than empires and more slow;
An hundred years should go to praise
Thine eyes, and on thy forehead gaze;

Two hundred to adore each breast,
But thirty thousand to the rest;
An age at least to every part,
And the last age should show your heart.
For, lady, you deserve this state,
Nor would I love at lower rate.
    But at my back I always hear
Time's wingèd chariot hurrying near,
And yonder all before us lie
Deserts of vast eternity.
Thy beauty shall no more be found,
Nor, in thy marble vault, shall sound
My echoing song; then worms shall try
That long-preserved virginity,
And your quaint honour turn to dust,
And into ashes all my lust:
The grave's a fine and private place,
But none, I think, do there embrace.
    Now therefore, while the youthful hue
Sits on thy skin like morning dew,
And while thy willing soul transpires
At every pore with instant fires,
Now let us sport us while we may,
And now, like amorous birds of prey,
Rather at once our time devour,
Than languish in his slow-chapt power.
Let us roll all our strength and all
Our sweetness up into one ball,
And tear our pleasures with rough strife,
Thorough the iron gates of life;
Thus, though we cannot make our sun
Stand still, yet we will make him run.

Andrew Marvell

VOICES AT THE WINDOW

Who is it that, this dark night,
   Underneath my window plaineth?
It is one who from thy sight
   Being, ah, exiled, disdaineth
Every other vulgar light.

Why, alas, and are you he?
   Be not yet those fancies changèd?
Dear, when you find change in me,
   Though from me you be estrangèd,
Let my change to ruin be.

Well, in absence this will die:
   Leave to see, and leave to wonder.
Absence sure will help, if I
   Can learn how myself to sunder
From what in my heart doth lie.

But time will these sad thoughts remove;
   Time doth work what no man knoweth,
Time doth as the subject prove:
   With time still the affection groweth
In the faithful turtle-dove.

What if you new beauties see?
   Will not they stir new affection?
I will think they pictures be
   (Image-like, of saints' perfection)
Poorly counterfeiting thee.

But your reason's purest light
   Bids you leave such minds to nourish.
Dear, do reason no such spite!
   Never doth thy beauty flourish
More than in my reason's sight.

                              Sir Philip Sidney

99

THE VOICE

Woman much missed, how you call to me, call to me,
Saying that now you are not as you were
When you had changed from the one who was all to me,
But as at first, when our day was fair.

Can it be you that I hear? Let me view you, then,
Standing as when I drew near to the town
Where you would wait for me: yes, as I knew you then,
Even to the original air-blue gown!

Or is it only the breeze, in its listlessness
Travelling across the wet mead to me here,
You being ever dissolved to existlessness
Heard no more again far or near?

   Thus I; faltering forward,
   Leaves around me falling,
Wind oozing thin through the thorn from norward,
   And the woman calling.

Thomas Hardy

A VALEDICTION FORBIDDING
MOURNING

As virtuous men pass mildly away,
   And whisper to their souls, to go,
Whilst some of their sad friends do say,
   The breath goes now, and some say, no:

So let us melt, and make no noise,
   No tear-floods, nor sigh-tempests move,
'Twere profanation of our joys
   To tell the laity our love.

Moving of th'earth brings harms and fears,
    Men reckon what it did and meant,
But trepidation of the spheres,
    Though greater far, is innocent.

Dull sublunary lovers' love
    (Whose soul is sense) cannot admit
Absence, because it doth remove
    Those things which elemented it.

But we by a love, so much refin'd,
    That ourselves know not what it is,
Inter-assurèd of the mind,
    Care less eyes, lips, and hands to miss.

Our two souls therefore, which are one,
    Though I must go, endure not yet
A breach, but an expansion,
    Like gold to aery thinness beat.

If they be two, they are two so
    As stiff twin compasses are two,
Thy soul the fixed foot, makes no show
    To move, but doth, if th'other do.

And though it in the centre sit,
    Yet when the other far doth roam,
It leans, and hearkens after it,
    And grows erect, as that comes home.

Such wilt thou be to me, who must
    Like th'other foot, obliquely run;
Thy firmness makes my circle just,
    And makes me end, where I begun.

                                    John Donne

From 'THE SPANISH FRIAR'

Farewell, ungrateful traitor!
  Farewell, my perjured swain!
Let never injured creature
  Believe a man again.
The pleasure of possessing
Surpasses all expressing,
But 'tis too short a blessing,
  And love too long a pain.

'Tis easy to deceive us,
  In pity of your pain;
But when we love, you leave us,
  To rail at you in vain.
Before we have descried it,
There is no bliss beside it,
But she, that once has tried it,
  Will never love again.

The passion you pretended,
  Was only to obtain;
But when the charm is ended,
  The charmer you disdain.
Your love by ours we measure,
Till we have lost our treasure;
But dying is a pleasure,
  When living is a pain.

John Dryden

From 'THE MAIDEN QUEEN'

I feed a flame within, which so torments me
That it both pains my heart, and yet contents me:
'Tis such a pleasing smart, and I so love it,
That I had rather die than once remove it.

Yet he for whom I grieve shall never know it;
My tongue does not betray, nor my eyes show it.
Not a sigh, not a tear, my pain discloses,
But they fall silently, like dew on roses.

Thus, to prevent my Love from being cruel,
My heart's the sacrifice, as 'tis the fuel;
And while I suffer this to give him quiet,
My faith rewards my love, though he deny it.

On his eyes will I gaze, and there delight me;
While I conceal my love no frown can fright me.
To be more happy I dare not aspire,
Nor can I fall more low, mounting no higher.

John Dryden

CONFESSIONS

What is he buzzing in my ears?
   'Now that I come to die,
Do I view the world as a vale of tears?'
   Ah, reverend sir, not I!

What I viewed there once, what I view again
   Where the physic bottles stand
On the table's edge, — is a suburb lane,
   With a wall to my bedside hand.

That lane sloped, much as the bottles do,
   From a house you could descry
O'er the garden wall: is the curtain blue
   Or green to a healthy eye?

To mine, it serves for the old June weather
   Blue above lane and wall;
And that farthest bottle labelled 'Ether'
   Is the house o'er-topping all

At a terrace, somewhat near its stopper,
 There watched for me, one June,
A girl: I know, sir, it's improper,
 My poor mind's out of tune.

Only, there was a way. . . you crept
 Close by the side, to dodge
Eyes in the house, two eyes except:
 They styled their house 'The Lodge.'

What right had a lounger up their lane?
 But, by creeping very close,
With the good wall's help, — their eyes might strain
 And stretch themselves to Oes,

Yet never catch her and me together,
 As she left the attic, there,
By the rim of the bottle labelled 'Ether,'
 And stole from stair to stair,

And stood by the rose-wreathed gate. Alas,
 We loved, sir — used to meet:
How sad and bad and mad it was —
 But then, how it was sweet!

                              Robert Browning

O WESTERN WIND

O Western wind, when wilt thou blow
 That the small rain down can rain?
Christ, that my love were in my arms
 And I in my bed again!

                              Anon.

5
COUNTRY PLEASURES

Happy the man whose wish and care
A few paternal acres bound,
Content to breathe his native air,
In his own ground

POPE

MY HEART'S IN THE HIGHLANDS

My heart's in the Highlands, my heart is not here;
My heart's in the Highlands a-chasing the deer;
Chasing the wild deer, and following the roe,
My heart's in the Highlands wherever I go.
Farewell to the Highlands, farewell to the North,
The birth-place of valour, the country of worth;
Wherever I wander, wherever I rove,
The hills of the Highlands for ever I love.

Farewell to the mountains high cover'd with snow;
Farewell to the straths and green valleys below;
Farewell to the forests and wild-hanging woods;
Farewell to the torrents and loud-pouring floods.
My heart's in the Highlands, my heart is not here;
My heart's in the Highlands a-chasing the deer;
Chasing the wild deer, and following the roe,
My heart's in the Highlands, wherever I go.

Robert Burns

A FARMER'S BOY

They strolled down the lane together,
The sky was studded with stars.
They reached the gate in silence,
And he lifted down the bars.
She neither smiled nor thanked him
Because she knew not how;
For he was just a farmer's boy
And she a Jersey cow. . .

Anon.

THE CUCKOO SINGS

When daisies pied and violets blue
  And lady-smocks all silver-white
And cuckoo-buds of yellow hue
  Do paint the meadows with delight,
The cuckoo then, on every tree,
Mocks married men; for thus sings he,
Cuckoo, cuckoo! — O word of fear,
Unpleasing to a married ear!

When shepherds pipe on oaten straws,
  And merry larks are ploughmen's clocks,
When turtles tread, and rooks, and daws,
  And maidens bleach their summer smocks,
The cuckoo then, on every tree,
Mocks married men; for thus sings he,
                Cuckoo!
Cuckoo, cuckoo! — O word of fear,
Unpleasing to a married ear!

William Shakespeare: Love's Labour's Lost

THE BROOK

I come from haunts of coot and hern,
  I make a sudden sally,
And sparkle out among the fern,
  To bicker down a valley.

By thirty hills I hurry down,
  Or slip between the ridges,
By twenty thorps, a little town,
  And half a hundred bridges.

Till last by Philip's farm I flow
  To join the brimming river,
For men may come and men may go,
  But I go on for ever.

I chatter over stony ways,
    In little sharps and trebles,
I bubble into eddying bays,
    I babble on the pebbles.

With many a curve my banks I fret
    By many a field and fallow,
And many a fairy foreland set
    With willow-weed and mallow.

I chatter, chatter, as I flow
    To join the brimming river,
For men may come and men may go,
    But I go on for ever.

I wind about, and in and out,
    With here a blossom sailing,
And here and there a lusty trout,
    And here and there a grayling,

And here and there a foamy flake
    Upon me, as I travel
With many a silvery waterbreak
    Above the golden gravel.

And draw them all along, and flow
    To join the brimming river,
For men may come and men may go,
    But I go on for ever.

I steal by lawns and grassy plots,
    I slide by hazel covers;
I move the sweet forget-me-nots
    That grow for happy lovers.

I slip, I slide, I gloom, I glance,
    Among my skimming swallows;
I make the netted sunbeam dance
    Against my sandy shallows.

I murmur under moon and stars
  In brambly wildernesses;
I linger by my shingly bars;
  I loiter round my cresses;

And out again I curve and flow
  To join the brimming river,
For men may come and men may go,
  But I go on for ever.

Alfred Tennyson

A BOY'S SONG

Where the pools are bright and deep,
Where the grey trout lies asleep,
Up the river and over the lea,
That's the way for Billy and me.

Where the blackbird sings the latest,
Where the hawthorn blooms the sweetest,
Where the nestlings chirp and flee,
That's the way for Billy and me.

Where the mowers mow the cleanest,
Where the hay lies thick and greenest,
There to track the homeward bee,
That's the way for Billy and me.

Where the hazel bank is steepest,
Where the shadow falls the deepest,
Where the clustering nuts fall free,
That's the way for Billy and me.

Why the boys should drive away,
Little sweet maidens from their play,
Or love to banter and fight so well,
That's the thing I never could tell.

But this I know, I love to play
Through the meadow, among the hay;
Up the water, and over the lea,
That's the way for Billy and me.

James Hogg

From 'L'ALLEGRO'

And, if I give thee honour due,
Mirth, admit me of thy crew,
To live with her, and live with thee,
In unreproved pleasures free;
To hear the lark begin his flight,
And, singing, startle the dull night,
From his watch-tower in the skies,
Till the dappled dawn doth rise;
Then to come, in spite of sorrow,
And at my window bid good-morrow,
Through the sweet-briar or the vine,
Or the twisted eglantine;
While the cock, with lively din,
Scatters the rear of darkness thin;
And to the stack, or the barn-door,
Stoutly struts his dames before:
Oft listening how the hounds and horn
Cheerly rouse the slumbering morn,
From the side of some hoar hill,
Through the high wood echoing shrill:
Sometime walking, not unseen,
By hedgerow elms, on hillocks green,
Right against the eastern gate
Where the great Sun begins his state,
Robed in flames and amber light,
The clouds in thousand liveries dight;
While the ploughman, near at hand,
Whistles o'er the furrowed land,
And the milkmaid singeth blithe,
And the mower whets his scythe,
And every shepherd tells his tale
Under the hawthorn in the dale.

John Milton

From 'THE SCHOLAR GYPSY'

Go, for they call you, Shepherd, from the hill;
Go, Shepherd, and untie the wattled cotes:
No longer leave thy wistful flock unfed,
Nor let thy bawling fellows rack their throats,
Nor the cropp'd grasses shoot another head.
But when the fields are still,
And the tired men and dogs all gone to rest,
And only the white sheep are sometimes seen
Cross and recross the strips of moon-blanch'd green;
Come, Shepherd, and again renew the quest.

Here, where the reaper was at work of late,
In this high field's dark corner, where he leaves
His coat, his basket, and his earthen cruise,
And in the sun all morning binds the sheaves,
Then here, at noon, comes back his stores to use;
Here will I sit and wait,
While to my ear from uplands far away
The bleating of the folded flocks is borne,
With distant cries of reapers in the corn —
All the live murmur of a summer's day.

Matthew Arnold

THE GARDEN

How vainly men themselves amaze,
To win the palm, the oak, or bays;
And their incessant labours see
Crowned from some single herb, or tree,
Whose short and narrow-vergèd shade
Does prudently their toils upbraid;
While all the flowers and trees do close,
To weave the garlands of repose!

Fair Quiet, have I found thee here,
And Innocence, thy sister dear?
Mistaken long, I sought you then
In busy companies of men.
Your sacred plants, if here below,
Only among the plants will grow;
Society is all but rude
To this delicious solitude.

No white nor red was ever seen
So amorous as this lovely green.
Fond lovers, cruel as their flame,
Cut in these trees their mistress' name:
Little, alas! they know or heed,
How far these beauties her's exceed!
Fair trees! wheres'e'er your bark I wound,
No name shall but your own be found.

When we have run our passion's heat,
Love hither makes his best retreat.
The gods, that mortal beauty chase,
Still in a tree did end their race;
Apollo hunted Daphne so,
Only that she might laurel grow;
And Pan did after Syrinx speed,
Not as a nymph, but for a reed.

What wondrous life is this I lead!
Ripe apples drop about my head;
The luscious clusters of the vine
Upon my mouth do crush their wine;
The nectarine, and curious peach,
Into my hands themselves do reach;
Stumbling on melons, as I pass,
Insnared with flowers, I fall on grass.

Meanwhile the mind, from pleasure less,
Withdraws into its happiness;
The mind, that ocean where each kind
Does straight its own resemblance find;
Yet it creates, transcending these,
Far other worlds, and other seas,
Annihilating all that's made
To a green thought in a green shade.

Here at the fountain's sliding foot,
Or at some fruit-tree's mossy root,
Casting the body's vest aside,
My soul into the boughs does glide;
There, like a bird, it sits and sings,
Then whets and combs its silver wings,
And, till prepared for longer flight,
Waves in its plumes the various light.

Such was that happy garden-state,
While man there walked without a mate:
After a place so pure and sweet,
What other help could yet be meet!
But 'twas beyond a mortal's share
To wander solitary there:
Two paradises 'twere in one,
To live in paradise alone.

How well the skilful gardener drew
Of flowers, and herbs, this dial new;
Where, from above, the milder sun
Does through a fragrant zodiac run,
And, as it works, the industrious bee
Computes its time as well as we!
How could such sweet and wholesome hours
Be reckoned but with herbs and flowers?

Andrew Marvell

THE REWARDS OF FARMING

Let the Wealthy and Great,
Roll in Splendour and State,
I envy them not, I declare it;
I eat my own Lamb,
My Chickens and Ham,
I shear my own Fleece and I wear it.
I have Lawns, I have Bow'rs,
I have Fruits, I have Flowers,
The Lark is my morning alarmer;
So jolly Boys now,
Here's God speed the Plough,
Long Life and Success to the Farmer!

Anon.

THE MARCH BEE

A warning wind finds out my resting-place
And in a mountain cloud the lost sun chills;
Night comes; and yet before she shows her face
The sun flings off the shadows, warm light fills
The valley and the clearings on the hills.
Bleak crow the moorcocks on the fen's blue plashes,
But here I warm myself with these bright looks and flashes.

And warmed like me the merry humble-bee
Puts fear aside, runs forth to catch the sun,
And by the ploughland's shoulder comes to see
The flowers that like him best, and seems to shun
Cold countless quaking wind-flowers every one,
Primroses too; but makes poor grass his choice
Where small wood-strawberry blossoms nestle and rejoice.

The magpies steering round from wood to wood,
Tree-creeper flickering up the elm's green rind,
Bold gnats that revel round my solitude
And most this pleasant bee intent to find
The new-born joy, inveigle the rich mind
Long after darkness comes cold-lipped to one
Still listening to the bee, still basking in the sun.

Edmund Blunden

FROM 'THE WINTER'S TALE'

When daffodils begin to peer,
  With hey! the doxy over the dale,
Why, then comes in the sweet o' the year;
  For the red blood reigns in the winter's pale.

The white sheet bleaching on the hedge,
  With hey! the sweet birds, O how they sing!
Doth set my pugging tooth on edge,
  For a quart of ale is a dish for a king.

The lark, that tirra-lirra chants,
  With hey! with hey! the thrush and the jay,
Are summer songs for me and my aunts,
  While we lie tumbling in the hay.

But shall I go mourn for that, my dear?
    The pale moon shines by night:
And when I wander here and there,
    I then do most go right.

If tinkers may have leave to live,
    And bear the sow-skin budget,
Then my account I well may give,
    And in the stocks avouch it.

William Shakespeare

116

MEG MERRILEES

Old Meg she was a Gipsy,
   And lived upon the Moors:
Her bed it was the brown heath turf,
   And her house was out of doors.

Her apples were swart blackberries,
   Her currants pods o'broom;
Her wine was dew of the wild white rose,
   Her book a churchyard tomb.

Her Brothers were the craggy hills,
   Her Sisters larchen trees —
Alone with her great family
   She lived as she did please.

No breakfast had she many a morn,
   No dinner many a noon,
And 'stead of supper she would stare
   Full hard against the Moon.

But every morn of woodbine fresh
   She made her garlanding,
And every night the dark glen Yew
   She wove, and she would sing.

And with her fingers old and brown
   She plaited Mats of Rushes,
And gave them to the Cottagers
   She met among the Bushes.

Old Meg was brave as Margaret Queen
   And tall as Amazon:
An old red blanket cloak she wore;
   A chip hat had she on.
God rest her aged bones somewhere —
   She died full long agone!

John Keats

WEATHERS

This is the weather the cuckoo likes,
　　And so do I;
When showers betumble the chestnut spikes,
　　And nestlings fly:
And the little brown nightingale bills his best,
And they sit outside at 'The Travellers' Rest,'
And maids come forth sprig-muslin drest,
And citizens dream of the south and west,
　　And so do I.

This is the weather the shepherd shuns,
　　And so do I;
When beaches drip in browns and duns,
　　And thresh, and ply;
And hill-hid tides throb, throe on throe,
And meadow rivulets overflow,
And drops on gate-bars hang in a row,
And rooks in families homeward go,
　　And so do I.

Thomas Hardy

ANSWER TO A CHILD'S QUESTION

Do you ask what the birds say?
　　The sparrow, the dove,
The linnet and thrush say,
　　'I love and I love!'

In the winter they're silent,
　　The wind is so strong;
What it says, I don't know,
　　But it sings a loud song.

But green leaves and blossoms,
    And sunny warm weather,
And singing and loving,
    All come back together.

But the lark is so brimful
    Of gladness and love,
The green fields below him,
    The blue sky above,

That he sings and he sings,
    And for ever sings he,
'I love my love,
    And my love loves me!'

Samuel Taylor Coleridge

CORINNA'S GOING A-MAYING

Get up, get up for shame! The blooming morn
    Upon her wings presents the god unshorn.
    See how Aurora throws her fair
    Fresh-quilted colours through the air:
    Get up, sweet slug-a-bed, and see
    The dew bespangling herb and tree!
Each flower has wept and bow'd toward the east
Above an hour since, yet you not drest;
    Nay! not so much as out of bed?
    When all the birds have matins said
    And sung their thankful hymns, 'tis sin,
    Nay, profanation, to keep in,
Whereas a thousand virgins on this day
Spring sooner than the lark, to fetch in May.

Rise and put on your foliage, and be seen
To come forth, like the spring-time, fresh and green,
 And sweet as Flora. Take no care
 For jewels for your gown or hair:
 Fear not; the leaves will strew
 Gems in abundance upon you:
Besides, the childhood of the day has kept,
Against you come, some orient pearls unwept.
 Come, and receive them while the light
 Hangs on the dew-locks of the night:
 And Titan on the eastern hill
 Retires himself, or else stands still
Till you come forth! Wash, dress, be brief in praying:
Few beads are best when once we go a-Maying.

Come, my Corinna, come; and coming, mark
How each field turns a street, each street a park,
 Made green and trimm'd with trees! see how
 Devotion gives each house a bough
 Or branch! each porch, each door, ere this,
 An ark, a tabernacle is,
Made up of white-thorn neatly interwove,
As if here were those cooler shades of love.
 Can such delights be in the street
 And open fields, and we not see't?
 Come, we'll abroad: and let's obey
 The proclamation made for May,
And sin no more, as we have done, by staying;
But, my Corinna, come, let's go a-Maying.

There's not a budding boy or girl this day
But is got up and gone to bring in May.
 A deal of youth ere this is come
 Back, and with white-thorn laden home.
 Some have despatch'd their cakes and cream,
 Before that we have left to dream:
And some have wept and woo'd, and plighted troth,

And chose their priest, ere we can cast off sloth:
    Many a green-grown has been given,
    Many a kiss, both odd and even:
    Many a glance, too, has been sent
    From out the eye, love's firmament:
Many a jest told of the keys betraying
This night, and locks pick'd: yet we're not a-Maying!

Come, let us go, while we are in our prime,
And take the harmless folly of the time!
    We shall grow old apace, and die
    Before we know our liberty.
    Our life is short, and our days run
    As fast away as does the sun.
And, as a vapour or a drop of rain,
Once lost, can ne'er be found again,
    So when or you or I are made
    A fable, song, or fleeting shade,
    All love, all liking, all delight
    Lies drown'd with us in endless night.
Then, while time serves, and we are but decaying,
Come, my Corinna, come, let's go a-Maying.

Robert Herrick

FLORAL TRIBUTE

(STIMULATED BY LISTENING TO A LAVEROCK OR LARK,
WHILE FISHING FOR A CHAVENDER OR CHUB)

The monkey-flower, or mimulus,
  The mimulus, or musk,
That grows beside the Imulus,
  The Imulus, or Usk,
Is humble and subfimulus,
  Is modestly subfusc.
Yet, when at evening dimulus,
  When at the falling dusk
I chew the bitter himulus
  Of life, the bitter husk —
Harder than any rimulus
  (A rimulus, or rusk),
Such as might crack a timulus,
  An elephantinc tusk —
Then to the stream I bimulus,
  All eagerly I busk,
To gaze on thee, O mimulus,
And from thee draw a stimulus,
  A stimulus, or stusk.

Sir Charles Jeffries

SUMMER

Winter is cold-hearted,
  Spring is yea and nay,
Autumn is a weathercock
  Blown every way.
Summer days for me
  When every leaf is on its tree;

122

When Robin's not a beggar,
   And Jenny Wren's a bride,
And larks hang singing, singing, singing,
   Over the wheat-fields wide,
   And anchored lilies ride,
And the pendulum spider
   Swings from side to side;

And blue-black bettles transact business,
   And gnats fly in a host,
And furry caterpillars hasten
   That no time be lost,
And moths grow fat and thrive,
   And ladybirds arrive.

Before green apples blush,
   Before green nuts embrown,
Why one day in the country
   Is worth a month in town;
Is worth a day and a year
Of the dusty, musty, lag-last fashion
That days drone elsewhere.

Christina Rossetti

ODE ON SOLITUDE

Happy the man whose wish and care
   A few paternal acres bound,
Content to breathe his native air,
   In his own ground.

Whose herds with milk, whose fields with bread,
   Whose flocks supply him with attire,
Whose trees in summer yield him shade,
   In winter fire.

Blest, who can unconcern'dly find
    Hours, days, and years slide soft away,
In health of body, peace of mind,
    Quiet by day,

Sound sleep by night; study and ease,
    Together mixt; sweet recreation;
And Innocence, which most does please
    With meditation.

Thus let me live, unseen, unknown,
    Thus unlamented let me die,
Steal from the world, and not a stone
    Tell where I lie.

Alexander Pope

THE GARDEN IN SEPTEMBER

Now thin mists temper the slow-ripening beams
Of the September sun: his golden gleams
On gaudy flowers shine, that prank the rows
Of high-grown hollyhocks, and all tall shows
That Autumn flaunteth in his bushy bowers;
Where tomtits, hanging from the drooping heads
Of giant sunflowers, peck the nutty seeds;
And in the feathery aster bees on wing
Seize and set free the honied flowers,
Till thousand stars leap with their visiting:
While ever across the path mazily flit,
Unpiloted in the sun,
The dreamy butterflies
With dazzling colours powdered and soft glooms,
White, black and crimson stripes, and peacock eyes,
Or on chance flowers sit,
With idle effort plundering one by one
The nectaries of deepest-throated blooms.

    With gentle flaws the western breeze
Into the garden saileth,

Scarce here and there stirring the single trees,
For his sharpness he vaileth:
So long a comrade of the bearded corn,
Now from the stubbles whence the shocks are borne,
O'er dewy lawns he turns to stray,
As mindful of the kisses and soft play
Wherewith he enamoured the light-hearted May,
Ere he deserted her;
Lover of fragrance, and too late repents;
Nor more of heavy hyacinth now may drink,
Nor spicy pink,
Nor summer's rose, nor garnered lavender,
But the few lingering scents
Of streakèd pea, and gillyflower, and stocks
Of courtly purple, and aromatic phlox.

And at all times to hear are drowsy tones
Of dizzy flies, and humming drones,
With sudden flap of pigeon wings in the sky,
Or the wild cry
Of thirsty rooks, that scour ascare
The distant blue, to watering as they fare
With creaking pinions, or — on business bent,
If aught their ancient polity displease, —
Come gathering to their colony, and there
Settling in ragged parliament,
Some stormy council hold in the high trees.

Robert Bridges

Tell me not here, it needs not saying,
  What tune the enchantress plays
In aftermaths of soft September
  Or under blanching mays,
For she and I were long acquainted
  And I knew all her ways.

On russet floors, by waters idle,
  The pine lets fall its cone;
The cuckoo shouts all day at nothing
  In leafy dells alone;
And traveller's joy beguiles in autumn
  Hearts that have lost their own.

On acres of the seeded grasses
    The changing burnish heaves;
Or marshalled under moons of harvest
    Stand still all night the sheaves;
Or beeches strip in storms for winter
    And stain the wind with leaves.

Possess, as I possessed a season,
    The countries I resign,
Where over elmy plains the highway
    Would mount the hills and shine,
And full of shade the pillared forest
    Would murmur and be mine.

For nature, heartless, witless nature,
    Will neither care nor know
What stranger's feet may find the meadow
    And trespass there and go,
Nor ask amid the dews of morning
    If they are mine or no.

                                    A E Housman

From 'THE TEMPEST'

Juno: Honour, riches, marriage – blessing,
Long continuance, and increasing,
Hourly joys be still upon you!
Juno sings her blessings on you.
Ceres: Earth's increase, foison plenty,
Barns and garners never empty,
Vines with clustering bunches growing,
Plants with goodly burden bowing;
Spring come to you, at the farthest,
In the very end of harvest!
Scarcity and want shall shun you;
Ceres' blessing so is on you.

                                William Shakespeare

TO AUTUMN

Season of mists and mellow fruitfulness,
    Close bosom-friend of the maturing sun;
Conspiring with him how to load and bless
    With fruit the vines that round the thatch-eaves run;
To bend with apples the moss'd cottage-trees,
    And fill all fruit with ripeness to the core;
        To swell the gourd, and plump the hazel shells
    With a sweet kernel; to set budding more,
And still more, later flowers for the bees,
Until they think warm days will never cease,
    For Summer has o'er-brimm'd their clammy cells.

Who hath not seen thee oft amid thy store?
    Sometimes whoever seeks abroad may find
Thee sitting careless on a granary floor,
    Thy hair soft-lifted by the winnowing wind;
Or on a half-reap'd furrow sound asleep,
    Drowsed with the fume of poppies, while thy hook
        Spares the next swath and all its twinèd flowers;
And sometimes like a gleaner thou dost keep
    Steady thy laden head across a brook;
    Or by a cider-press, with patient look,
        Thou watchest the last oozings hours by hours.

Where are the songs of Spring? Ay, where are they?
    Think not of them, thou hast thy music too, —
While barrèd clouds bloom the soft-dying day,
    And touch the stubble-plains with rosy hue;
Then in a wailful choir the small gnats mourn
    Among the river sallows, borne aloft
        Or sinking as the light wind lives or dies;
And full-grown lambs loud bleat from hilly bourn;
    Hedge-crickets sing; and now with treble soft
    The red-breast whistles from a garden-croft;
        And gathering swallows twitter in the skies.

John Keats

6
COME AND TRIP IT
AS YOU GO

Tasting of Flora and the country green,
Dance, and Provençal song, and sunburnt mirth!

KEATS

THE FIDDLER OF DOONEY

When I play on my fiddle in Dooney,
Folk dance like a wave of the sea;
My cousin is priest in Kilvarnet,
My brother in Mocharabuiee.

I passed my brother and cousin:
They read in their books of prayer;
I read in my book of songs
I bought at the Sligo fair.

When we come at the end of time
To Peter sitting in state,
He will smile on the three old spirits,
But call me first through the gate;

For the good are always the merry,
Save by an evil chance,
And the merry love the fiddle,
And the merry love to dance:

And when the folk there spy me,
They will all come up to me,
With 'Here is the fiddler of Dooney!'
And dance like a wave of the sea.

William Butler Yeats

ON HER DANCING

I stood and saw my Mistress dance,
Silent, and with so fixed an eye,
Some might suppose me in a trance:
    But being askèd why,
By one who knew I was in love,
    I could not but impart
My wonder, to behold her move
So nimbly with a marble heart.

James Shirley

SONG

The merchant, to secure his treasure,
   Conveys it in a borrow'd name:
Euphelia serves to grace my measure;
   But Chloe is my real flame.

My softest verse, my darling lyre,
   Upon Euphelia's toilet lay;
When Chloe noted her desire
   That I should sing, that I should play.

My lyre I tune, my voice I raise;
   But with my numbers mix my sighs:
And while I sing Euphelia's praise,
   I fix my soul on Chloe's eyes.

Fair Chloe blush'd: Euphelia frown'd:
   I sung, and gazed: I play'd, and trembled:
And Venus to the Loves around
   Remark'd, how ill we all dissembled.

Matthew Prior

From 'THE TEMPEST'

Ariel: Come unto these yellow sands,
   And then take hands:
Curtsied when you have, and kist
   The wild waves whist:
Foot it featly here and there,
And sweet sprites the burden bear.
   Hark, hark,
     Bow-wow:
   The watch-dogs bark,
     Bow-wow.
   Hark, hark, I hear
   The strain of strutting chanticleer
   Cry cockadidle-do.

William Shakespeare

131

DRINKING SONG

I have been in love, and in debt, and in drink,
   This many and many a year!
And those are three plagues enough, any should think,
   For one poor mortal to bear!
'Twas love made me fall into drink;
   And drink made me run into debt!
And though I have struggled, and struggled and strove;
   I cannot get out of them yet!

There's nothing but money can cure me;
   And rid me of all my pain!
     'Twill pay all my debts;
     And remove all my lets;
And my Mistress that cannot endure me,
   Will love me and love me again!
Then I'll fall to my loving and drinking amain.

Alexander Brome

FANCY'S KNELL

When lads were home from labour
   At Abdon under Clee,
A man would call his neighbour
   And both would send for me.
And where the light in lances
   Across the mead was laid,
There to the dances
   I fetched my flute and played.

Ours were idle pleasures,
   Yet oh, content we were,
The young to wind the measures,
   The old to heed the air;

And I to lift with playing
    From tree and tower and steep
The light delaying,
    And flute the sun to sleep.

The youth toward his fancy
    Would turn his brow of tan,
And Tom would pair with Nancy
    And Dick step off with Fan;
The girl would lift her glances
    To his, and both be mute:
Well went the dances
    At evening to the flute.

Wenlock Edge was umbered,
    And bright was Abdon Burf,
And warm between them slumbered
    The smooth green miles of turf;
Until from grass and clover
    The upshot beam would fade,
And England over
    Advanced the lofty shade.

The lofty shade advances,
    I fetch my flute and play:
Come, lads, and learn the dances
    And praise the tune today.
To-morrow, more's the pity,
    Away we both must hie,
To air the ditty,
    And to earth I.

A.E. Housman

LACHLAN GORACH'S RHYME

First the heel,
And then the toe,
That's the way
The polka goes.

First the toe,
And then the heel,
That's the way
To dance a reel.

Quick about,
And then away,
Lightly dance
The glad Strathspey.

Jump a jump,
And jump it big,
That's the way
To dance a jig.

Slowly, smiling,
As in France,
Follow through
The country dance.

Anon.

A LOBSTER QUADRILLE

'Will you walk a little faster?' said a whiting to a snail,
'There's a porpoise close behind us, and he's treading on
  my tail.
See how eagerly the lobsters and the turtles all advance!
They are waiting on the shingle — will you come and join the
  dance?

Will you, won't you, will you, won't you, will you join the
    dance?
Will you, won't you, will you, won't you, won't you join the
    dance?

'You can really have no notion how delightful it will be
When they take us up and throw us, with the lobsters, out
    to sea!'
But the snail replied 'Too far, too far!' and gave a look
    askance —
Said he thanked the whiting kindly, but he would not join
    the dance.
Would not, could not, would not, could not, would not join
    the dance.
Would not, could not, would not, could not, could not join
    the dance.

'What matters it how far we go?' his scaly friend replied,
'There is another shore, you know, upon the other side.
The further off from England the nearer is to France —
Then turn not pale, beloved snail, but come and join the
    dance.
Will you, won't you, will you, won't you, will you join the
    dance?
Will you, won't you, will you, won't you, won't you join
    the dance?'

Lewis Carroll

PIPING DOWN THE VALLEYS WILD

Piping down the valleys wild,
    Piping songs of pleasant glee,
On a cloud I saw a child,
    And he laughing said to me:

'Pipe a song about a Lamb!'
   So I piped with merry cheer.
'Piper, pipe that song again';
   So I piped: he wept to hear.

'Drop thy pipe, thy happy pipe;
   Sing thy songs of happy cheer':
So I sang the same again,
   While he wept with joy to hear.

'Piper, sit thee down and write
   In a book, that all may read."
So he vanished from my sight,
   And I plucked a hollow reed,

And I made a rural pen,
   And I stained the water clear,
And I wrote my happy songs
   Every child may joy to hear.

William Blake

CHORUS FROM 'ATALANTA'

When the hounds of spring are on winter's traces,
   The mother of months in meadow or plain
Fills the shadows and windy places
   With lisp of leaves and ripple of rain;
And the brown bright nightingale amorous
Is half assuaged for Itylus,
For the Thracian ships and the foreign faces,
   The tongueless vigil, and all the pain.

Come with bows bent and with emptying of quivers,
   Maiden most perfect, lady of light,
With a noise of winds and many rivers,
   With a clamour of waters, and with might;
Bind on thy sandals, O thou most fleet,
Over the splendour and speed of thy feet;

For the faint east quickens, the wan west shivers,
    Round the feet of the day and the feet of the night.

Where shall we find her, how shall we sing to her,
    Fold our hands round her knees, and cling?
O that man's heart were as fire and could spring to her,
    Fire, or the strength of the streams that spring!
For the stars and the winds are unto her
As raiment, as songs of the harp-player;
For the risen stars and the fallen cling to her,
    And the southwest-wind and the west-wind sing.

For winter's rains and ruins are over,
    And all the season of snows and sins;
The days dividing lover and lover,
    The light that loses, the night that wins;
And time remember'd is grief forgotten,
And frosts are slain and flowers begotten,
And in green underwood and cover
    Blossom by blossom the spring begins.

The full streams feed on flower of rushes,
    Ripe grasses trammel a travelling foot,
The faint fresh flame of the young year flushes
    From leaf to flower and flower to fruit;
And fruit and leaf are as gold and fire,
And the oat is heard above the lyre,
And the hoofèd heal of a satyr crushes
    The chestnut-husk at the chestnut-root.

And Pan by noon and Bacchus by night,
    Fleeter of foot than the fleet-foot kid,
Follows with dancing and fills with delight
    The Maenad and the Bassarid;
And soft as lips that laugh and hide
The laughing leaves of the trees divide,
And screen from seeing and leave in sight
    The god pursuing, the maiden hid.

The ivy falls with the Bacchanal's hair
  Over her eyebrows hiding her eyes;
The wild vine slipping down leaves bare
  Her bright breast shortening into sighs;
The wild vine slips with the weight of its leaves,
But the berried ivy catches and cleaves
To the limbs that glitter, the feet that scare
  The wolf that follows, the fawn that flies.

Algernon Charles Swinburne

DRINKING

The thirsty earth soaks up the rain,
And drinks and gapes for drink again;
The plants suck in the earth, and are
With constant drinking fresh and fair;
The sea itself (which one would think
Should have but little need of drink)
Drinks twice ten thousand rivers up,
So fill'd that they o'erflow the cup.
The busy Sun (and one would guess
By 's drunken fiery face no less)
Drinks up the sea, and when he's done,
The Moon and Stars drink up the Sun;
They drink and dance by their own light,
They drink and revel all the night:
Nothing in Nature's sober found,
But an eternal health goes round.
Fill up the bowl, then, fill it high,
Fill all the glasses there — for why
Should every creature drink but I?
Why, man of morals, tell me why?

Abraham Cowley

If all the world were paper,
And all the seas were ink;
If all the trees were bread and cheese,
How should we do for drink?

If there had been no heroes,
Nor none that did great wrongs;
If fiddlers should turn farmers all,
How should we do for songs?

If all things were eternal,
And nothing their end bringing;
If this should be, then how should we,
Here make an end of singing?

Anon.

'LET US DRINK AND BE MERRY'

Let us drink and be merry, dance, joke, and rejoice,
With claret and sherry, theorbo and voice!
The changeable world to our joy is unjust,
    All treasure's uncertain,
    Then down with your dust!
In frolics dispose your pounds, shillings, and pence,
For we shall be nothing a hundred years hence.

We'll sport and be free with Moll, Betty, and Dolly,
Have oysters and lobsters to cure melancholy:
Fish-dinners will make a man spring like a flea,
    Dame Venus, love's lady,
    Was born of the sea;
With her and with Bacchus we'll tickle the sense,
For we shall be past it a hundred years hence.

Your most beautiful bride who with garlands is crown'd
And kills with each glance as she treads on the ground,
Whose lightness and brightness doth shine in such splendour
    That none but the stars
    Are thought fit to attend her,
Though now she be pleasant and sweet to the sense,
Will be damnable mouldy a hundred years hence.

Then why should we turmoil in cares and in fears,
Turn all our tranquill'ty to sighs and to tears?
Let's eat, drink, and play till the worms do corrupt us,
    'Tis certain, *Post mortem*
    Nulla Voluptas.
For health, wealth and beauty, wit, learning and sense,
Must all come to nothing a hundred years hence.

Thomas Jordan

7

WHITHER, O SPLENDID SHIP

Where great whales come sailing by,
Sail and sail, with unshut eye,
Round the world for ever and aye

MATTHEW ARNOLD

From 'THE SAILOR'S CONSOLATION'

One night came on a hurricane,
The sea was mountains rolling,
When Barney Buntline turned his quid
And said to Billy Bowling:
'A strong sou'-wester's blowing, Billy,
Can't you hear it roar now?
Lord help 'em, how I pities all
Unhappy folks on shore now!

'And often have we seamen heard
How men are killed or undone
By overturns in carriages,
And thieves, and fires, in London;
We've heard what risks all landsmen run,
From noblemen to tailors;
So, Billy, let's thank Providence
That you and I are sailors.'

Anon.

CAWSAND BAY

In Cawsand Bay lying, with the Blue Peter flying,
   And all hands on deck for the anchor to weigh,
When off came a lady, as fresh as a daisy,
   And modestly hailing, the damsel did say:

'Ship ahoy! bear a hand there! I wants a young
      man there,
   So heave us a man-rope, or send him to me;
His name's Henry Grady, and I am a lady,
   Arrived to prevent him from going to sea.'

Now the captain, his honour, when he looked upon her,
   He ran down the side for to hand her on board.
Cried he, with emotion, 'What son of the ocean
   Can thus be looked after by Helena Ford?'

142

Then the lady made answer, 'That there is a man, sir,
    I'll make him as free as a Duke or a Lord.' —
'Oh no!' says the capp'en, 'That can't very well happen,
    I've got sailing orders — you, sir, stop on board.'

But up spoke the lady, 'Don't you mind him, Hal Grady,
    He once was your capp'en, but now you're at large.
You shan't stop on board her, for all that chap's order!'
    Then out of her bosom she drew his discharge.

Said the captain, 'I'm hang'd now, you're cool, and I'm
      bang'd now!'
Said Hal, 'Here, old Weatherface, take all my clothes.'
And ashore then he steer'd her; the lads they all cheer'd
    her:
But the captain was jealous, and looked down his nose.

Then she got a shore tailor to rig up her sailor
    In white nankeen trowsers and long blue-tail'd coat;
And he looked like a squire, for all to admire,
    With a dimity handkercher tied round his throat.

They'd a house that was greater than any first-rater,
    With footmen in livery handing the drink,
And a garden to go in, where flowers were blowing,
    The buttercup, daisy, the lily, the pink.

And he got edication befitting his station
    (For we all of us know we're not too old to larn);
And his messmates they found him, his little ones round
    him,
All chips of the old block from the stem to the starn.

                              Anon.

IN ROMNEY MARSH

As I went down to Dymchurch Wall,
    I heard the South sing o'er the land;
I saw the yellow sunlight fall
    On knolls where Norman churches stand.

And ringing shrilly, taut and lithe,
    Within the wind a core of sound,
The wire from Romney town to Hythe
    Alone its airy journey wound.

A veil of purple vapour flowed
    And trailed its fringe along the Straits;
The upper air like sapphire glowed;
    And roses filled Heaven's central gates.

Masts in the offing wagged their tops;
    The swinging waves pealed on the shore;
The saffron beach, all diamond drops
    And beads of surge, prolonged the roar.

As I came up from Dymchurch Wall,
    I saw above the Downs' low crest
The crimson brands of sunset fall,
    Flicker and fade from out the west.

Night sank: like flakes of silver fire
    The stars in one great shower came down;
Shrill blew the wind; and shrill the wire
    Rang out from Hythe to Romney town.

The darkly shining salt sea drops
    Streamed as the waves clashed on the shore;
The beach, with all its organ stops
    Pealing again, prolonged the roar.

John Davidson

THE INCHCAPE ROCK

No stir in the air, no stir in the sea,
The ship was still as she could be,
Her sails from heaven received no motion,
Her keel was steady in the ocean.

Without either sign or sound of their shock
The waves flow'd over the Inchcape Rock;
So little they rose, so little they fell,
They did not move the Inchcape Bell.

The worthy Abbot of Aberbrothock
Had placed that bell on the Inchcape Rock,
On a buoy in the storm it floated and swung,
And over the waves its warning rung.

When the Rock was hid by the surge's swell,
The mariners heard the warning bell;
And then they knew the perilous Rock,
And bless'd the Abbot of Aberbrothock.

The sun in heaven was shining gay,
All things were joyful on that day;
The sea-birds scream'd as they wheel'd round,
And there was joyaunce in the sound.

The buoy of the Inchcape Bell was seen,
A darker speck on the ocean green;
Sir Ralph the Rover walk'd his deck,
And he fixed his eye on the darker speck.

He felt the cheering power of spring,
It made him whistle, it made him sing;
His heart was mirthful to excess,
But the Rover's mirth was wickedness.

His eye was on the Inchcape float,
Quoth he, 'My men, put out the boat,
And row me to the Inchcape Rock,
And I'll plague the Abbot of Aberbrothock.'

The boat is lowered, the boatmen row,
And to the Inchcape Rock they go;
Sir Ralph bent over from the boat,
And he cut the Bell from the Inchcape float.

Down sank the Bell with a gurgling sound,
The bubbles arose and burst around;
Quoth Sir Ralph, 'The next who comes to the Rock
Won't bless the Abbot of Aberbrothock.'

Sir Ralph the Rover sail'd away,
He scour'd the seas for many a day;
And now grown rich with plunder'd store,
He steers his course for Scotland's shore.

So thick a haze o'erspreads the sky
They cannot see the sun on high;
The wind hath blown a gale all day,
At evening it hath died away.

On deck the Rover takes his stand,
So dark it is they see no land;
Quoth Sir Ralph, 'It will be lighter soon,
For there is the dawn of the rising Moon.'

'Canst hear,' said one, 'the breakers roar?
For methinks we should be near the shore.'
'Now where we are I cannot tell,
But I wish I could hear the Inchcape Bell.'

They hear no sound, the swell is strong;
Though the wind hath fallen they drift along,
Till the vessel strikes with a shivering shock, —
'Oh Christ! it is the Inchcape Rock!'

Sir Ralph the Rover tore his hair;
He curst himself in his despair;
But the waves rush in on every side,
And the vessel sinks beneath the tide.

Robert Southey

THE SHIP OF RIO

There was a ship of Rio
  Sailed out into the blue,
And nine and ninety monkeys
  Were all her jovial crew.
From bo'sun to the cabin boy,
  From quarter to caboose,
There weren't a stitch of calico
  To breech 'em — tight or loose;
From spar to deck, from deck to keel,
  From barnacle to shroud,
There weren't one pair of reach-me-downs
  To all that jabbering crowd.
But wasn't it a gladsome sight,
  When roared the deep-sea gales,
To see them reef her fore and aft,
  A-swinging by their tails!
Oh, wasn't it a gladsome sight,
  When glassy calm did come,
To see them squatting tailor-wise
  Around a keg of rum!
Oh, wasn't it a gladsome sight,
  When in she sailed to land,
To see them all a-scampering skip
  For nuts across the sand!

Walter de la Mare

LITTLE BILLEE

There were three sailors of Bristol city
Who took a boat and went to sea,

But first with beef and captain's biscuits
And pickled pork they loaded she.

There was gorging Jack and guzzling Jimmy,
And youngest he was little Billee.

Now when they got as far as the Equator
They'd nothing left but one split pea.

Says gorging Jack to guzzling Jimmy,
'I am extremely hungaree.'

To gorging Jack says guzzling Jimmy,
'We've nothing left; us must eat we.'

Says gorging Jack to guzzling Jimmy,
'With one another we shouldn't agree!

There's little Bill, he's young and tender,
We're old and tough, so let's eat he.'

'Oh, Bill, we're going to kill and eat you,
So undo the button of your chemie.'

When Bill received this information
He used his pocket handkerchie.

'First let me say my catechism,
Which my poor mammy taught to me.'

'Make haste, make haste,' says guzzling Jimmy,
While Jack pulled out his snickersnee.

So Billy went up to the main-top gallant mast,
And down he fell on his bended knee,

He scarce had come to the twelfth commandment
When up he jumps. 'There's land I see:

'There's Jerusalem and Madagascar,
And North and South Amerikee:

'There's the British flag a-riding at anchor,
With Admiral Napier, K.C.B.'

So when they got aboard the Admiral's,
He hanged fat Jack and flogged Jimmee:

But as for little Bill, he made him
The Captain of a Seventy-three.

W M Thackeray

MY BONNIE MARY

Go fetch to me a pint o' wine,
   An' fill it in a silver tassie,
That I may drink, before I go,
   A service to my bonnie lassie.
The boat rocks at the pier o' Leith,
   Fu' loud the wind blaws frae the ferry,
The ship rides by the Berwick-law,
   And I maun leave my bonnie Mary.

The trumpets sound, the banners fly,
   The glittering spears are rankèd ready;
The shouts o' war are heard afar,
   The battle closes thick and bloody;
But it's no the roar o' sea or shore
   Wad mak me langer wish to tarry;
Nor shout o' war that's heard afar —
   It's leaving thee, my bonnie Mary!

Robert Burns

TO LUCASTA, GOING BEYOND THE SEAS

If to be absent were to be
    Away from thee;
  Or that when I am gone
  You or I were alone;
Then, my Lucasta, might I crave
Pity from blustering wind or swallowing wave.

But I'll not sigh one blast or gale
    To swell my sail,
  Or pay a tear to 'suage
  The foaming blue god's rage;
For whether he will let me pass
Or no, I'm still as happy as I was.

Though seas and land betwixt us both,
    Our faith and troth,
  Like separated souls,
  All time and space controls:
Above the highest sphere we meet
Unseen, unknown; and greet as Angels greet.

So then we do anticipate
    Our after-fate,
  And are alive i' the skies,
  If thus our lips and eyes
Can speak like spirits unconfined
In heaven, their earthy bodies left behind.

Richard Lovelace

THE FORSAKEN MERMAN

Come, dear children, let us away;
  Down and away below.
Now my brothers call from the bay;
Now the great winds shoreward blow;
Now the salt tides seaward flow;
Now the wild white horses play,
Champ and chafe and toss in the spray.
  Children dear, let us away.
    This way, this way.

Call her once before you go.
    Call once yet.
In a voice that she will know:
  'Margaret! Margaret!'
Children's voices should be dear
(Call once more) to a mother's ear:
Children's voices, wild with pain.
Surely she will come again.
Call her once and come away.
    This way, this way.
'Mother dear, we cannot stay.'
The wild white horses foam and fret.
  Margaret! Margaret!

Come, dear children, come away down.
    Call no more.
One last look at the white-wall'd town,
And the little grey church on the windy shore.
    Then come down.
She will not come though you call all day.
    Come away, come away.
Children dear, was it yesterday
We heard the sweet bells over the bay?
In the caverns where we lay,
Through the surf and through the swell,
The far-off sound of a silver bell?

Sand-strewn caverns, cool and deep,
Where the winds are all asleep;
Where the spent lights quiver and gleam;
Where the salt weed sways in the stream;
Where the sea-beasts ranged all round
Feed in the ooze of their pasture-ground;
Where the sea-snakes coil and twine,
Dry their mail and bask in the brine;
Where great whales come sailing by,
Sail and sail, with unshut eye,
Round the world for ever and aye?
When did music come this way?
Children dear, was it yesterday?

   Children dear, was it yesterday
   (Call yet once) that she went away?
   Once she sate with you and me,
On a red gold throne in the heart of the sea,
   And the youngest sate on her knee.
She comb'd its bright hair, and she tended it well,
When down swung the sound of the far-off bell.
She sigh'd, she look'd up through the clear green sea.
She said, 'I must go, for my kinsfolk pray
In the little grey church on the shore today.
'Twill be Easter-time in the world — ah me!
And I lose my poor soul, Merman, here with thee.'
I said, 'Go up, dear heart, through the waves,
Say thy prayer, and come back to the kind sea-caves.'
She smiled, she went up through the surf in the bay.
   Children dear, was it yesterday?
   Children dear, were we long alone?
'The sea grows stormy, the little ones moan.
Long prayers,' I said, 'in the world they say.
Come,' I said, and we rose through the surf in the bay.
We went up the beach, by the sandy down
Where the sea-stocks bloom, to the white-wall'd town.
Through the narrow paved streets, where all was still,
To the little grey church on the windy hill.

From the church came a murmur of folk at their prayers,
But we stood without in the cold-blowing airs.
We climb'd on the graves, on the stones worn with rains,
And we gazed up the aisle through the small leaded panes.
    She sate by the pillar; we saw her clear:
    'Margaret, hist! come quick, we are here.
    Dear heart,' I said, 'we are long alone.
    The sea grows stormy, the little ones moan.'
But, ah! she gave me never a look,
For her eyes were seal'd to the holy book.
Loud prays the priest; shut stands the door.
    Come away, children, call no more.
    Come away, come down, call no more.

        Down, down, down.
    Down to the depths of the sea.
She sits at her wheel in the humming town,
    Sining most joyfully.
Hark what she sings: 'O joy, O joy,
For the humming street, and the child with its toy,
For the priest, and the bell, and the holy well.
    For the wheel where I spun,
    And the blessèd light of the sun.'
    And so she sings her fill,
    Singing most joyfully,
    Till the shuttle falls from her hand,
    And the whizzing wheel stands still.
She steals to the window, and looks at the sand;
    And over the sand at the sea;
    And her eyes are set in a stare;
    And anon there breaks a sigh,
    And anon there drops a tear,
    From a sorrow-clouded eye,
    And a heart sorrow-laden,
        A long, long sigh
For the cold strange eyes of a little Mermaiden,
    And the gleam of her golden hair.

Come away, away children.
Come children, come down.
The hoarse wind blows colder;
Lights shine in the town.
She will start from her slumber
When gusts shake the door;
She will hear the winds howling,
Will hear the waves roar.
We shall see, while above us
The waves roar and whirl,
A ceiling of amber,
A pavement of pearl.
Singing, 'Here came a mortal,
But faithless was she;
And alone dwell for ever
The kings of the sea.'

But, children, at midnight,
When soft the winds blow;
When clear falls the moonlight;
When spring-tides are low:
When sweet airs come seaward
From heaths starr'd with broom;
And high rocks throw mildly
On the blanch'd sands a gloom:
Up the still, glistening beaches,
Up the creeks we will hie;
Over banks of bright seaweed
The ebb-tide leaves dry.
We will gaze, from the sand-hills,
At the white, sleeping town;
At the church on the hill-side —
    And then come back down.
Singing, 'There dwells a loved one,
    But cruel is she,
She left lonely for ever
    The kings of the sea.'

Matthew Arnold

FISHERMAN'S SONG

O blithely shines the bonnie sun
Upon the Isle o' May,
And blithely rolls the morning tide
Into St. Andrews bay.

When haddocks leave the Firth o' Forth,
And mussels leave the shore,
When oysters climb up Berwick Law,
We'll go to sea no more,
No more,
We'll go to sea no more!

Anon.

THE SIRENS' SONG

Steer, hither steer your winged pines,
    All beaten mariners!
Here lie Love's undiscover'd mines,
    A prey to passengers —
Perfumes far sweeter than the best
Which makes the Phoenix' urn and nest.
    Fear not your ships,
Nor any to oppose you save our lips;
    But come on shore,
Where no joy dies till Love hath gotten more.

For swelling waves our panting breasts,
    Where never storms arise,
Exchange, and be awhile our guests:
    For stars gaze on our eyes.
The compass Love shall hourly sing,
And as he goes about the ring,
    We will not miss
To tell each point he nameth with a kiss.
    — Then come on shore,
Where no joy dies till Love hath gotten more.

William Browne

155

From 'THE TEMPEST'

Stephano: The master, the swabber, the boat-swain and I,
The gunner, and his mate,
Loved Mall, Meg, and Marian, and Margery,
But none of us cared for Kate.
For she had a tongue with a tang,
Would cry to a sailor, Go hang!
She loved not the savour of tar nor of pitch,
Yet a tailor might scratch her where'er she did itch,
Then to sea, boys, and let her go hang!

William Shakespeare

A PASSER-BY

Whither, O splendid ship, thy white sails crowding,
   Leaning across the bosom of the urgent West,
That fearest nor sea rising, nor sky clouding,
   Whither away, fair rover, and what thy quest?
   Ah! soon, when Winter has all our vales opprest,
When skies are cold and misty, and hail is hurling,
   Wilt thou glide on the blue Pacific, or rest
In a summer haven asleep, thy white sails furling.

I there before thee, in the country that well thou knowest,
   Already arrived am inhaling the odorous air:
I watch thee enter unerringly where thou goest,
   And anchor queen of the strange shipping there,
   Thy sails for awnings spread, thy masts bare;
Nor is aught from the foaming reef to the snow-capped,
     grandest
   Peak, that is over the feathery palms more fair
Than thou, so upright, so stately, and still thou standest.

And yet, O splendid ship, unhailed and nameless,
   I know not if, aiming a fancy, I rightly divine
That thou hast a purpose joyful, a courage blameless,
   Thy port assured in a happier land than mine.

But for all I have given thee, beauty enough is thine,
As thou, aslant with trim tackle and shrouding,
  From the proud nostril curve of a prow's line
In the offing scatterest foam, thy white sails crowding.

Robert Bridges

A CINQUE PORT

Below the down the stranded town
  What may betide forlornly waits,
With memories of smoky skies
  When Gallic navies crossed the straits;
When waves with fire and blood grew bright,
And cannon thundered through the night.

With swinging stride the rhythmic tide
  Bore to the harbour barque and sloop;
Across the bar the ship of war,
  In castled stern and lanterned poop,
Came up with conquests on her lee,
The stately mistress of the sea.

Where argosies have wooed the breeze,
  The simple sheep are feeding now;
And near and far across the bar
  The ploughman whistles at the plough;
Where once the long waves washed the shore,
Larks from their lowly lodgings soar.

Below the down the stranded town
  Hears far away the rollers beat;
About the wall the seabirds call;
  The salt wind murmurs through the street;
Forlorn the sea's forsaken bride
Awaits the end that shall betide.

John Davidson

MEETING AT NIGHT

The grey sea and the long black land;
And the yellow half-moon large and low;
And the startled little waves that leap
In fiery ringlets from their sleep,
As I gain the cove with pushing prow,
And quench its speed in the slushy sand.

Then a mile of warm sea-scented beach;
Three fields to cross till a farm appears;
A tap at the pane, the quick sharp scratch
And blue spurt of a lighted match,
And a voice less loud, thro' its joys and fears,
Than the two hearts beating each to each!

Robert Browning

THE STORM
From Letter to Mr. Christopher Brooke

But when I waked, I saw that I saw not;
I, and the sun, which should teach me, had forgot
East, west, day, night; and I could only say,
If the world had lasted, now it had been day.
Thousands our noises were, yet we 'mongst all
Could none by his right name, but thunder call:
Lightning was all our light, and it rained more
Than if the sun had drunk the sea before.
Some coffined in their cabins lie, equally
Grieved that they are not dead, and yet must die;
And as sin-burdened souls from graves will creep
At the last day, some forth their cabins peep,
And tremblingly ask, 'What news?' and do hear so,
Like jealous husbands, what they would not know.
Some, sitting on the hatches, would seem there
With hideous gazing to fear away fear.

Then note they the ship's sicknesses, the mast
Shaked with this ague, and the hold and waist
With a salt dropsy clogged, and all our tacklings
Snapping, like too-high-stretch'd treble strings.
And as sin-burdened souls from graves will creep,
At the last day, some forth their cabins peep:
Even our ordnance, placed for our defence,
Strive to break loose, and 'scape away from thence.
Pumping hath tired our men, and what's the gain?
Seas into seas thrown, we suck in again;
Hearing hath deafed our sailors; and if they
Knew how to hear, there's none knows what to say.
Compared to these storms, death is but a qualm,
Hell somewhat lightsome, and the Bermuda calm.
Darkness, light's elder brother, his birth-right
Claims o'er this world, and to heaven hath chased light.
All things are one, and that one none can be,
Since all forms uniform deformity
Doth cover, so that we, except God say
Another *Fiat*, shall have no more day.
So violent, yet long, these furies be,
That though thine absence starve me, I wish not thee.

John Donne

A DRIFTER OFF TARENTUM

He from the wind-bitten North with ship and companions
    descended,
Searching for eggs of death spawned by invisible hulls.
Many he found and drew forth. Of a sudden the fishery ended
In flame and a clamorous breath known to the eye-pecking
    gulls.

Rudyard Kipling

159

From 'THE TEMPEST'

Ariel: Full fathom five thy father lies,
Of his bones are coral made:
Those are pearls that were his eyes;
Nothing of him that doth fade,
But doth suffer a sea-change
Into something rich, and strange:
Sea-nymphs hourly ring his knell.
     Ding dong.
Hark now I hear them, ding-dong bell.

                    William Shakespeare

FOR MUSIC

There be none of Beauty's daughters
   With a magic like thee;
And like music on the waters
   Is thy sweet voice to me:
When, as if its sound were causing
The charmèd ocean's pausing,
The waves lie still and gleaming,
And the lull'd winds seem dreaming:

And the midnight moon is weaving
   Her bright chain o'er the deep;
Whose breast is gently heaving,
   As an infant's asleep:
So the spirit bows before thee,
To listen and adore thee;
With a full but soft emotion,
Like the swell of Summer's ocean.

                    Lord Byron

THE 'GOLDEN VANITY'

A ship I have got in the North Country
And she goes by the name of the *Golden Vanity,*
O I fear she'll be taken by a Spanish Ga-la-lee,
    As she sails by the Low-lands low.

To the Captain then upspake the little Cabin-boy,
He said, 'What is my fee, if the galley I destroy?
The Spanish Ga-la-lee, if no more it shall anoy,
    As you sail by the Low-lands low.'

'Of silver and of gold I will give to you a store;
And my pretty little daughter that dwelleth on the shore,
Of treasure and of fee as well, I'll give to thee galore,
    As we sail by the Low-lands low.'

Then they row'd him up tight in a black bull's skin,
And he held all in his hand an augur sharp and thin,
And he swam until he came to the Spanish Gal-a-lin,
    As she lay by the Low-lands low.

He bored with his augur, he bored once and twice,
And some were playing cards, and some were playing dice,
When the water flowed in it dazzled their eyes,
    And she sank by the Low-lands low.

So the Cabin-boy did swim all to the larboard side,
Saying 'Captain! take me in, I am drifting with the tide!'
'I will shoot you! I will kill you!' the cruel Captain cried,
    'You may sink by the Low-lands low.'

Then the Cabin-boy did swim all to the starboard side,
Saying, 'Messmates, take me in, I am drifting with the tide!'
Then they laid him on the deck, and he closed his eyes and
    died,
    As they sailed by the Low-lands low.

161

They sew'd his body tight in an old cow's hide,
And they cast the gallant Cabin-boy out over the ship side,
And left him without more ado to drift with the tide,
    And to sink by the Low-lands low.

Anon.

THE SANDS OF DEE

'O Mary, go and call the cattle home,
    And call the cattle home,
    And call the cattle home,
Across the sands of Dee.'
The western wind was wild and dank with foam,
    And all alone went she.

The western tide crept up along the sand,
    And o'er and o'er the sand,
    And round and round the sand,
As far as eye could see.
The rolling mist came down and hid the land:
    And never home came she.

'Oh! is it weed, or fish or floating hair –
    A tress of golden hair,
    A drowned maiden's hair,
Above the nets at sea?'
Was never salmon yet that shone so fair
    Among the stakes of Dee.

They rowed her in across the rolling foam,
    The cruel crawling foam,
    The cruel hungry foam,
To her grave beside the sea.
But still the boatmen hear her call the cattle home,
    Across the sands of Dee.

Charles Kingsley

SONG

The boat is chafing at our long delay,
   And we must leave too soon
The spicy sea-pinks and the inborne spray,
   The tawny sands, the moon.

Keep us, O Thetis, in our western flight!
   Watch from thy pearly throne
Our vessel, plunging deeper into night
   To reach a land unknown.

John Davidson

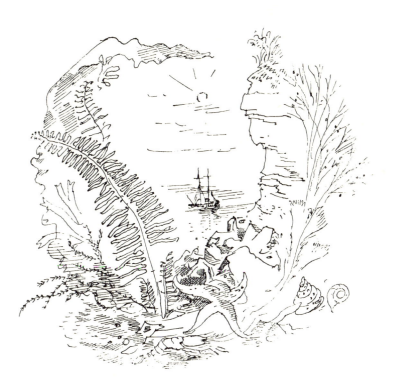

THE OLD SHIPS

I have seen old ships sail like swans asleep
Beyond the village which men still call Tyre,
With leaden age o'ercargoed, dipping deep
For Famagusta and the hidden sun
That rings black Cyprus with a lake of fire;
And all those ships were certainly so old —
Who knows how oft with squat and noisy gun,
Questing brown slaves or Syrian oranges,
The pirate Genoese
Hell-raked them till they rolled
Blood, water, fruit and corpses up the hold.
But now through friendly seas they softly run,
Painted the mid-sea blue or shore-sea green,
Still patterned with the vine and grapes in gold.

But I have seen
Pointing her shapely shadows from the dawn
An image tumbled on a rose-swept bay
A drowsy ship of some yet older day;
And, wonder's breath indrawn,
Thought I — who knows — who knows — but in that same
(Fished up beyond Aeaea, patched up new
— Stern painted brighter blue —)
That talkative, bald-headed seaman came
(Twelve patient comrades sweating at the oar)
From Troy's doom-crimson shore,
And with great lies about his wooden horse
Set the crew laughing, and forgot his course.

It was so old a ship — who knows, who knows?
— And yet so beautiful, I watched in vain
To see the mast burst open with a rose,
And the whole deck put on its leaves again.

James Elroy Flecker

8

IF WISHES WERE HORSES

If wishes were horses,
Beggars would ride;
If turnips were watches,
I would wear one by my side

ANON

HORSES

Those lumbering horses in the steady plough,
On the bare field - I wonder why, just now,
They seemed terrible, so wild and strange,
Like magic power on the stony grange.

Perhaps some childish hour has come again,
When I watched fearful, through the blackening rain,
Their hooves like pistons in an ancient mill
Move up and down, yet seem as standing still.

Their conquering hooves which trod the stubble down
Were ritual that turned the field to brown,
And their great hulks were seraphim of gold,
Or mute ecstatic monsters on the mould.

And oh the rapture, when, one furrow done,
They marched broad-breasted to the sinking sun!
The light flowed off their bossy sides in flakes;
The furrows rolled behind like struggling snakes.

But when at dusk with steaming nostrils home
They came, they seemed gigantic in the gloam,
And warm and glowing with mysterious fire
That lit their smouldering bodies in the mire.

Their eyes as brilliant and as wide as night
Gleamed with a cruel apocalyptic light.
Their manes the leaping ire of the wind
Lifted with rage invisible and blind.

Ah, now it fades! it fades! and I must pine
Again for that dread country crystalline,
Where the blank field and the still-standing tree
Were bright and fearful presences to me.

Edwin Muir

HORSES ON THE CAMARGUE

In the grey wastes of dread,
The haunt of shattered gulls where nothing moves
But in a shroud of silence like the dead,
I heard a sudden harmony of hooves,
And, turning, saw afar
A hundred snowy horses unconfined,
The silver runaways of Neptune's car
Racing, spray-curled, like waves before the wind.
Sons of the Mistral, fleet
As him with whose strong gusts they love to flee,
Who shod the flying thunders on their feet
And plumed them with the snortings of the sea;
Theirs is no earthly breed
Who only haunt the verges of the earth
And only on the sea's salt herbage feed —
Surely the great white breakers gave them birth.
For when for years a slave,
A horse of the Camargue, in alien lands,
Should catch some far-off fragrance of the wave
Carried far inland from his native sands,
Many have told the tale
Of how in fury, foaming at the rein,
He hurls his rider; and with lifted tail,
With coal-red eyes and cataracting mane,
Heading his course for home,
Though sixty foreign leagues before him sweep,
Will never rest until he breathes the foam
And hears the native thunder of the deep.
But when the great gusts rise
And lash their anger on these arid coasts,
When the scared gulls career with mournful cries
And whirl across the waste like driven ghosts:
When hail and fire converge,
The only souls to which they strike no pain
Are the white-crested fillies of the surge
And the white horses of the windy plain.

Then in their strength and pride
The stallions of the wilderness rejoice;
They feel their Master's trident in their side,
And high and shrill they answer to his voice.
With white tails smoking free,
Long streaming manes, and arching necks, they show
Their kinship to their sisters of the sea —
And forward hurl their thunderbolts of snow.
Still out of hardship bred,
Spirits of power and beauty and delight
Have ever on such frugal pastures fed
And loved to course with tempests through the night.

Roy Campbell

A SMUGGLER'S SONG

If you wake at midnight, and hear a horse's feet,
Don't go drawing back the blind, or looking in the street.
Them that asks no questions isn't told a lie.
Watch the wall, my darling, while the Gentlemen go by!
    Five and twenty ponies,
    Trotting through the dark —
    Brandy for the Parson,
    'Baccy for the Clerk;
  Laces for a lady, letters for a spy,
And watch the wall, my darling, while the Gentlemen go by!

Running round the woodlump if you chance to find
Little barrels, roped and tarred, all full of brandy-wine,
Don't you shout to come and look, nor use 'em for your play.
Put the brushwood back again, — and they'll be gone next day!

If you see the stable-door setting open wide;
If you see a tired horse lying down inside;
If your mother mends a coat cut about and tore;
If the lining's wet and warm — don't you ask no more!

If you meet King George's men, dressed in blue and red,
You be careful what you say, and mindful what is said.
If they call you 'pretty maid', and chuck you 'neath the chin,
Don't you tell where no one is, nor yet where no one's been!

Knocks and footsteps round the house - whistles after dark —
You've no call for running out till the house-dogs bark.
Trusty's here, and *Pincher's* here, and see how dumb they lie —
They don't fret to follow when the Gentlemen go by!

If you do as you've been told, 'likely there's a chance
You'll be give a dainty doll, all the way from France,
With a cap of Valenciennes, and a velvet hood —
A present from the Gentlemen, along o' being good!
    Five and twenty ponies,
    Trotting through the dark —
    Brandy for the Parson,
    'Baccy for the Clerk;
Them that asks no questions isn't told a lie —
Watch the wall, my darling, while the Gentlemen go by!

Rudyard Kipling

THE NUTCRACKERS AND THE SUGAR-TONGS

The Nutcrackers sate by a plate on the table,
  The Sugar-tongs sate by a plate at his side;
And the Nutcrackers said, 'Don't you wish we were able
  Along the blue hills and green meadows to ride?
Must we drag on this stupid existence for ever,
  So idle and weary, so full of remorse, —
While every one else takes his pleasure, and never
  Seems happy unless he is riding a horse?

Don't you think we could ride without being instructed?
  Without any saddle, or bridle, or spur?
Our legs are so long, and so aptly constructed,
  I'm sure that an accident could not occur.
Let us all of a sudden hop down from the table,
  And hustle downstairs, and each jump on a horse!
Shall we try? Shall we go? Do you think we are able?'
  The Sugar-tongs answered distinctly, 'Of course!'

So down the long staircase they hopped in a minute,
  The Sugar-tongs snapped, and the Crackers said 'crack!'
The stable was open, the horses were in it;
  Each took out a pony, and jumped on his back.
The Cat in a fright scrambled out of the doorway,
  The Mice tumbled out of a bundle of hay,
The brown and white Rats, and the black ones from Norway,
Screamed out, 'They are taking the horses away!'

The whole of the household was filled with amazement,
  The Cups and the Saucers danced madly about,
The Plates and the Dishes looked out of the casement,
  The Saltcellar stood on his head with a shout,
The Spoons with a clatter looked out of the lattice,
  The Mustard-pot climbed up the Gooseberry Pies,
The Soup-ladle peeped through a heap of Veal Patties,
  And squeaked with a ladle-like scream of surprise.

The Frying-pan said, 'It's an awful delusion!'
    The Tea-kettle hissed and grew black in the face;
And they all rushed downstairs in the wildest confusion,
    To see the great Nutcracker-Sugar-tong race.
And out of the stable, with screamings and laughter
    (Their ponies were cream-coloured, speckled with brown,)
The Nutcrackers first, and the Sugar-tongs after,
    Rode all round the yard, and then all round the town.

They rode through the street, and they rode by the station,
    They galloped away to the beautiful shore;
In silence they rode, and 'made no observation,'
    Save this: 'We will never go back any more!'
And still you might hear, till they rode out of hearing,
    The Sugar-tongs snap, and the Crackers say 'crack!'
Till far in the distance their forms disappearing,
    They faded away. — And they never came back!

                                        Edward Lear

THE DIVERTING HISTORY
OF JOHN GILPIN

John Gilpin was a citizen
    of credit and renown,
A train-band captain eke was he
    Of famous London town.

John Gilpin's spouse said to her dear:
    'Though wedded we have been
These twice ten tedious years, yet we
    No holiday have seen.

'To-morrow is our wedding-day,
    And we will then repair
Unto the Bell at Edmonton
    All in a chaise and pair.

'My sister, and my sister's child,
    Myself, and children three,
Will fill the chaise; so you must ride
    On horseback after we.'

He soon replied: 'I do admire
    Of womankind but one,
And you are she, my dearest dear,
    Therefore, it shall be done.

'I am a linen-draper bold,
    As all the world doth know,
And my good friend the calender
    Will lend his horse to go.'

Quoth Mrs. Gilpin: 'That's well said:
    And; for that wine is dear,
We will be furnished with our own,
    Which is both bright and clear.'

John Gilpin kissed his loving wife;
    O'erjoyed was he to find
That, though on pleasure she was bent,
    She had a frugal mind.

The morning came, the chaise was brought,
    But yet was not allowed
To drive up to the door, lest all
    Should say that she was proud.

So three doors off the chaise was stayed,
    Where they did all get in;
Six precious souls, and all agog
    To dash through thick and thin!

Smack went the whip, round went the wheels,
    Were never folk so glad;
The stones did rattle underneath,
    As if Cheapside were mad.

John Gilpin at his horse's side
  Seized fast the flowing mane,
And up he got, in haste to ride,
  But soon came down again;

For saddle-tree scarce reached had he,
  His journey to begin,
When, turning round his head, he saw
  Three customers come in.

So down he came; for loss of time,
  Although it grieved him sore,
Yet loss of pence, full well he knew,
  Would trouble him much more.

'Twas long before the customers
  Were suited to their mind,
When Betty screaming came down stairs:
  'The wine is left behind!'

'Good lack!' quoth he — 'yet bring it me,
  My leathern belt likewise,
In which I bear my trusty sword
  When I do exercise.'

Now Mrs. Gilpin — careful soul! —
  Had two stone-bottles found,
To hold the liquor that she loved,
  And keep it safe and sound.

Each bottle had a curling ear,
  Through which the belt he drew,
And hung a bottle on each side,
  To make his balance true.

Then over all, that he might be
  Equipped from top to toe,
His long red cloak, well brushed and neat,
  He manfully did throw.

Now see him mounted once again
  Upon his nimble steed,
Full slowly pacing o'er the stones
  With caution and good heed.

But finding soon a smoother road
  Beneath his well-shod feet,
The snorting beast began to trot,
  Which galled him in his seat.

So, 'Fair and softly,' John he cried,
  But John he cried in vain;
That trot became a gallop soon,
  In spite of curb and rein.

So stooping down, as needs he must
  Who cannot sit upright,
He grasped the mane with both his hands,
  And eke with all his might.

His horse, who never in that sort
  Had handled been before,
What thing upon his back had got
  Did wonder more and more.

Away went Gilpin, neck or nought;
  Away went hat and wig!
He little dreamt, when he set out,
  Of running such a rig!

The wind did blow, the cloak did fly,
  Like streamer long and gay,
Till, loop and button failing both,
  At last it flew away.

Then might all people well discern
  The bottles he had slung;
A bottle swinging at each side,
  As hath been said or sung.

The dogs did bark, the children screamed,
  Up flew the windows all;
And every soul cried out: 'Well done!'
  As loud as he could bawl.

Away went Gilpin — who but he?
  His fame soon spread around;
He carries weight! he rides a race!
  'Tis for a thousand pound!

And still, as fast as he drew near,
  'Twas wonderful to view
How in a trice the turnpike-men
  Their gates wide open threw.

And now, as he went bowing down
  His reeking head full low,
The bottles twain behind his back
  Were shattered at a blow.

Down ran the wine into the road,
  Most piteous to be seen,
Which made his horse's flanks to smoke
  As they had basted been.

But still he seemed to carry weight,
  With leathern girdle braced;
For all might see the bottle-necks
  Still dangling at his waist.

Thus all through merry Islington
  These gambols he did play,
Until he came unto the Wash
  Of Edmonton so gay.

And there he threw the wash about
  On both sides of the way,
Just like unto a trundling mop,
  Or a wild goose at play.

At Edmonton his loving wife
From the balcony spied
Her tender husband, wondering much
To see how he did ride.

'Stop, stop, John Gilpin! — Here's the house' —
They all at once did cry;
'The dinner waits, and we are tired:'
Said Gilpin: 'So am I!'

But yet his horse was not a whit
Inclined to tarry there;
For why? his owner had a house
Full ten miles off, at Ware.

So like an arrow swift he flew,
Shot by an archer strong;
So did he fly — which brings me to
The middle of my song.

Away went Gilpin, out of breath,
And sore against his will,
Till at his friend the calender's
His horse at last stood still.

The calender, amazed to see
His neighbour in such trim,
Laid down his pipe, flew to the gate,
And thus accosted him:

'What news? what news? your tidings tell;
Tell me you must and shall —
Say why bareheaded you are come,
Or why you come at all?'

Now Gilpin had a pleasant wit,
And loved a timely joke;
And thus unto the calender
In merry guise he spoke:

'I came because your horse would come;
    And, if I well forbode,
My hat and wig will soon be here —
    They are upon the road.'

The calender, right glad to find
    His friend in merry pin,
Returned him not a single word,
    But to the house went in;

Whence straight he came with hat and wig;
    A wig that flowed behind,
A hat not much the worse for wear,
    Each comely in its kind.

He held them up, and in his turn,
    Thus showed his ready wit:
'My head is twice as big as yours,
    They therefore needs must fit.

'But let me scrape the dirt away
    That hangs upon your face;
And stop and eat, for well you may
    Be in a hungry case.'

Said John: 'It is my wedding-day,
    And all the world would stare,
If wife should dine at Edmonton
    And I should dine at Ware!'

So, turning to his horse, he said:
    'I am in haste to dine;
'Twas for your pleasure you came here,
    You shall go back for mine.'

Ah, luckless speech, and bootless boast!
    For which he paid full dear;
For, while he spake, a braying ass
    Did sing most loud and clear;

Whereat his horse did snort, as he
  Had heard a lion roar,
And galloped off with all his might,
  As he had done before.

Away went Gilpin, and away
  Went Gilpin's hat and wig!
He lost them sooner than at first;
  For why? — they were too big.

Now Mistress Gilpin, when she saw
  Her husband posting down
Into the country far away,
  She pulled out half-a-crown;

And thus unto the youth she said
  That drove them to the Bell:
'This shall be yours when you bring back
  My husband safe and well."

The youth did ride, and soon did meet
  John coming back amain;
Whom in a trice he tried to stop,
  By catching at his rein;

But, not performing what he meant,
  And gladly would have done,
The frighted steed he frighted more,
  And made him faster run.

Away went Gilpin, and away
  Went post-boy at his heels!
The post-boy's horse right glad to miss
  The lumbering of the wheels.

Six gentlemen upon the road,
  Thus seeing Gilpin fly,
With post-boy scampering in the rear,
  They raised the hue and cry:

'Stop thief! stop thief! — a highwayman'
    Not one of them was mute;
And all and each that passed that way
    Did join in the pursuit.

And now the turnpike gates again
    Flew open in short space;
The toll-men thinking, as before,
    That Gilpin rode a race.

And so he did, and won it too,
    For he got first to town;
Nor stopped till where he had got up
    He did again get down.

Now let us sing, long live the king,
    And Gilpin, long live he;
And, when he next doth ride abroad,
    May I be there to see!

                            William Cowper

From 'KING RICHARD II'

Groom: I was a poor groom of thy stable, king,
When thou wert king; who, traveling towards York,
With much ado at length have gotten leave
To look upon my sometimes royal master's face:
O, how it erned my heart when I beheld,
In London streets that coronation day,
When Bolingbroke rode on roan Barbary!
That horse that thou so often hast bestrid,
That horse that I so carefully have dressed!
Richard: Rode he on Barbary? tell me, gentle friend,
How went he under him?
Groom: So proudly as if he disdained the ground.
Richard: So proud that Bolingbroke was on his back. . .

That jade hath eat bread from my royal hand,
This hand hath made him proud with clapping him:
Would he not stumble? would he not fall down,
Since pride must have a fall, and break the neck
Of that proud man that did usurp his back?
Forgiveness, horse! why do I rail on thee,
Since thou, created to be awed by man,
Wast born to bear? I was not made a horse,
And yet I bear a burthen like an ass,
Spurred, galled, and tired by jauncing Bolingbroke.

William Shakespeare

From 'VENUS AND ADONIS'

But lo, from forth a copse that neighbours by,
A breeding jennet, lusty, young and proud,
Adonis' trampling courser doth espy,
And forth she rushes, snorts and neighs aloud.
   The strong-necked steed, being tied unto a tree,
   Breaketh his rein and to her straight goes he.

Imperiously he leaps, he neighs, he bounds,
And now his woven girths he breaks asunder;
The bearing earth with his hard hoof he wounds,
Whose hollow womb resounds like heaven's thunder;
   The iron bit he crusheth 'tween his teeth,
   Controlling what he was controlléd with.

His ears up-pricked; his braided hanging mane
Upon his compassed crest now stand on end;
His nostrils drink the air, and forth again,
As from a furnace, vapours doth he send;
   His eye, which scornfully glisters like fire,
   Shows his hot courage and his high desire.

Sometime he trots, as if he told the steps,
With gentle majesty and modest pride;

Anon he rears upright, curvets and leaps,
As who should say 'Lo, thus my strength is tried,
　　And this I do to captivate the eye
　　Of the fair breeder that is standing by.'

What recketh he his rider's angry stir,
His flattering 'Holla' or his 'Stand, I say'?
What cares he now for curb or pricking spur?
For rich caparisons or trappings gay?
　　He sees his love, and nothing else he sees,
　　For nothing else with his proud sight agrees.

Look when a painter would surpass the life
In limning out a well-proportionéd steed,
His art with nature's workmanship at strife,
As if the dead the living should exceed;
　　So did this horse excel a common one
　　In shape, in courage, colour, pace and bone.

Round-hoofed, short-jointed, fetlocks shag and long,
Broad breast, full eye, small head and nostril wide,
High crest, short ears, straight legs and passing strong,
Thin mane, thick tail, broad buttock, tender hide;
　　Look what a horse should have he did not lack,
　　Save a proud rider on so proud a back.

Sometime he scuds far off, and there he stares;
Anon he starts at stirring of a feather;
To bid the wind a base he now prepares,
And whe'er he run or fly they know not whether;
　　For through his mane and tail the high wind sings,
　　Fanning the hairs, who wave like feath'red wings.

He looks upon his love and neighs unto her;
She answers him as if she knew his mind;
Being proud, as females are, to see him woo her,
She puts on outward strangeness, seems unkind,
　　Spurns at his love and scorns the heat he feels,
　　Beating his kind embracements with her heels.

Then, like a melancholy malcontent,
He vails his tail, that, like a falling plume,
Cool shadow to his melting buttock lent;
He stamps, and bites the poor flies in his fume.
　　His love, perceiving how he was enraged,
　　Grew kinder, and his fury was assuaged.

William Shakespeare

PEGASUS

It was there on the hillside, no tall traveller's story.
A cloud caught on a whin-bush, an airing of bleached
Linen, a swan, the cliff of a marble quarry –
It could have been any of these: but as he approached,
He saw that it was indeed what he had cause
Both to doubt and believe in – a horse, a winged white horse.

It filled the pasture with essence of solitude.
The wind tiptoed away like an interloper,
The sunlight there became a transparent hood
Estranging what it revealed; and the bold horse-coper,
The invincible hero, trudging up Helicon,
Knew he had never before been truly alone.

It stood there, solid as ivory, dreamy as smoke;
Or moved, and its hooves went dewdropping so lightly
That even the wild cyclamen were not broken:
But when those hooves struck rock, such was their might
They tapped a crystal vein which flowed into song
As it ran through thyme and grasses down-along.

'Pegasus,' he called, 'Pegasus' – with the surprise
Of one for the first time naming his naked lover.
The creature turned its lordly, incurious eyes
Upon the young man; but they seemed to pass him over
As something beneath their pride or beyond their ken.
It returned to cropping the violets and cyclamen.

Such meekness, indifference frightened him more than any
Rumoured Chimaera. He wavered, remembering how
This milk-white beast was born from the blood of uncanny
Medusa, the nightmare-eyed: and at once, although
Its brief glance had been mild, he felt a cringing
And pinched himself to make sure he was not changing

Into a stone. The animal tossed its head;
The white mane lifted and fell like an arrogant whinny.
'Horses are meant to be ridden,' the hero said,
'Wings or no wings, and men to mount them. Athene
'Ordered my mission, besides, and certainly you
'Must obey that goddess,' he cried, and flung the lassoo.

The cyclamen bow their heads, the cicadas pause.
The mountain shivers from flank to snowy top,
Shaking off eagles as a pastured horse
Shakes off a cloud of flies. The faint airs drop.
Pegasus, with a movement of light on water,
Shimmers aside, is elsewhere, mocking the halter.

So there began the contest. A young man
Challenging, coaxing, pursuing, always pursuing
The dream of those dewfall hooves: a horse which ran
Quicksilver from his touch, sliding and slewing
Away, then immobile a moment, derisively tame,
Almost as if it entered into a game.

He summoned up his youth, his conscious art
To tire or trick the beast, criss-crossing the meadow
With a web of patient moves, circling apart,
Nearing, and pouncing, but only upon its shadow.
What skill and passion weave the subtle net!
But Pegasus goes free, unmounted yet.

All day he tried for this radiant creature. The more he
Persevered, the less he thought of the task
For which he required it, and the ultimate glory.
So it let him draw close, closer — nearly to grasp

Its mane; but that instant it broke out wings like a spread
Of canvas, and sailed off easily overhead.

He cursed Pegasus then. Anger arose
With a new desire, as if it were some white girl
To stretch, mount, master, exhaust in shuddering throes.
The animal gave him a different look: it swirled
Towards him, circled him round in a dazzling mist,
And one light hoof just knocked upon his breast.

The pale sky yawns to its uttermost concave,
Flowers open their eyes, rivulets prance
Again, and over the mountainside a wave
Of sparkling air tumbles. Now from its trance
That holy ground is deeply sighing and stirring.
The heights take back their eagles, cicadas are whirring.

The furious art, the pursuer's rhythmic pace
Failed in him now. Another self had awoken,
Which knew — but felt no chagrin, no disgrace —
That he, not the winged horse, was being broken:
It was his lode, his lord, his appointed star,
He but its shadow and familiar.

So he lay down to sleep. Argos, Chimaera,
Athene in one solution were immersed.
Around him, on bush and blade, each dewdrop mirrored
A star, his riding star, his universe,
While on the moonlit flowers at his side
Pegasus grazed, palpable, undenied.

A golden bridle came to him in sleep —
A mesh of immortal fire and sensual earth,
Pliant as love, compulsive as the sweep
Of light-years, brilliant as truth, perfect as death.
He dreamed a magic bridle, and next day
When he awoke, there to his hand it lay.

Wings furled, on printless feet through the dews of morn
Pegasus stepped, in majesty and submission,
Towards him. Mane of tempest, delicate mien,
It was all brides, all thoroughbreds, all pent passion.
Breathing flowers upon him, it arched a superb
Neck to receive the visionary curb.

Pegasus said, 'The bridle that you found
'In sleep, you yourself made. Your hard pursuit,
'Your game with me upon this hallowed ground
'Forged it, your failures tempered it. I am brute
'And angel. He alone, who taps the source
'Of both, can ride me. Bellerophon, I am yours.'

C Day Lewis

AS THE TEAM'S HEAD-BRASS

As the team's head-brass flashed out on the turn
The lovers disappeared into the wood.
I sat among the boughs of the fallen elm
That strewed an angle of the fallow, and
Watched the plough narrowing a yellow square
Of charlock. Every time the horses turned
Instead of treading me down, the ploughman leaned
Upon the handles to say or ask a word,
About the weather, next about the war.
Scraping the share he faced towards the wood,
And screwed along the furrow till the brass flashed
Once more.
        The blizzard felled the elm whose crest
I sat in, by a woodpecker's round hole,
The ploughman said. 'When will they take it away?'
'When the war's over.' So the talk began —
One minute and an interval of ten,
A minute more and the same interval.

'Have you been out?' 'No.' 'And don't want to, perhaps?'
'If I could only come back again, I should.
I could spare an arm. I shouldn't want to lose
A leg. If I should lose my head, why, so,
I should want nothing more. . . Have many gone
From here?' 'Yes.' 'Many lost?' 'Yes: good few.
Only two teams work on the farm this year.
One of my mates is dead. The second day
In France they killed him. It was back in March,
The very night of the blizzard, too. Now if
He had stayed here we should have moved the tree.'
'And I should not have sat here. Everything
Would have been different. For it would have been
Another world.' 'Ay, and a better, though
If we could see all all might seem good.' Then
The lovers came out of the wood again:
The horses started and for the last time
I watched the clods crumble and topple over
After the ploughshare and the stumbling team.

Edward Thomas

FELIX RANDAL

Felix Randal the farrier, O he is dead then? my duty all
   ended,
Who have watched his mould of man, big-boned and hardy-
   handsome
Pining, pining, till time when reason rambled in it and some
Fatal four disorders, fleshed there, all contended?

Sickness broke him. Impatient he cursed at first, but mended
Being anointed and all; though a heavenlier heart began some
Months earlier, since I had our sweet reprieve and ransom
Tendered to him. Ah well, God rest him all road ever he
   offended!

This seeing the sick endears them to us, us too it endears.
My tongue had taught thee comfort, touch had quenched
   thy tears,
Thy tears that touched my heart, child, Felix, poor Felix
   Randal;

How far from then forethought of, all thy more boisterous
   years,
When thou at the random grim forge, powerful amidst peers,
Didst fettle for the great grey drayhorse his bright and
   battering sandal!

                                    Gerard Manley Hopkins

9

THE ANATOMY
OF MELANCHOLY

We're all in the dumps,
For diamonds are trumps,
The kittens are gone to St. Paul's
The babies are bit,
The moon's in a fit
And the houses are built without walls

ANON

MELANCHOLY

Hence, all you vain delights,
   As short as are the nights
Wherein you spend your folly!
There's naught in this life sweet,
If men were wise to see't,
   But only melancholy —
   O sweetest melancholy!
Welcome, folded arms and fixèd eyes,
A sight that piercing mortifies,
A look that's fasten'd to the ground,
A tongue chain'd up without a sound!

Fountain-heads and pathless groves,
Places which pale passion loves!
Moonlight walks, when all the fowls
Are warmly housed, save bats and owls!
   A midnight bell, a parting groan —
   These are the sounds we feed upon:
Then stretch our bones in a still gloomy valley,
Nothing's so dainty sweet as lovely melancholy.

John Fletcher

FOUR DUCKS ON A POND

Four ducks on a pond,
A grass bank beyond,
A blue sky of spring,
White clouds on the wing;
What a little thing
To remember for years —
To remember with tears.

William Allingham

THE SOLITARY REAPER

Behold her, single in the field,
  Yon solitary Highland Lass!
Reaping and singing by herself;
  Stop here, or gently pass!
Alone she cuts and binds the grain,
And sings a melancholy strain;
O listen! for the Vale profound
Is overflowing with the sound.

No Nightingale did ever chaunt
  More welcome notes to weary bands
Of travellers in some shady haunt,
  Among Arabian sands:
A voice so thrilling ne'er was heard
In spring-time from the Cuckoo-bird,
Breaking the silence of the seas
Among the farthest Hebrides.

Will no one tell me what she sings? —
  Perhaps the plaintive numbers flow
For old, unhappy, far-off things,
  And battles long ago:
Or is it some more humble lay,
Familiar matter of to-day?
Some natural sorrow, loss, or pain,
That has been, and may be again?

Whate'er the theme, the Maiden sang
  As if her song could have no ending;
I saw her singing at her work,
  And o'er the sickle bending; —
I listen'd, motionless and still;
And, as I mounted up the hill,
The music in my heart I bore,
Long after it was heard no more.

William Wordsworth

PIANO

Softly, in the dusk, a woman is singing to me;
Taking me back down the vista of years, till I see
A child sitting under the piano, in the boom of the tingling
   strings
And pressing the small, poised feet of a mother who smiles
   as she sings.

In spite of myself, the insidious mastery of song
Betrays me back, till the heart of me weeps to belong
To the old Sunday evenings at home, with winter outside
And hymns in the cosy parlour, the tinkling piano our guide.

So now it is vain for the singer to burst into clamour
With the great black piano appassionato. The glamour
Of childish days is upon me, my manhood is cast
Down in the flood of remembrance, I weep like a child for
   the past.

D.H. Lawrence

TEARS

It seems I have no tears left. They should have fallen —
Their ghosts, if tears have ghosts, did fall — that day
When twenty hounds streamed by me, not yet combed out
But still all equals in their rage of gladness
Upon the scent, made one, like a great dragon
In Blooming Meadow that bends towards the sun
And once bore hops: and on that other day
When I stepped out from the double-shadowed Tower
Into an April morning, stirring and sweet
And warm. Strange solitude was there and silence.
A mightier charm than any in the Tower
Possessed the courtyard. They were changing guard,
Soldiers in line, young English countrymen,
Fair-haired and ruddy, in white tunics. Drums
And fifes were playing 'The British Grenadiers.'
The men, the music piercing that solitude
And silence, told me truths I had not dreamed,
And have forgotten since their beauty passed.

Edward Thomas

MARIANA

With blackest moss the flower-pots
    Were thickly crusted, one and all:
The rusted nails fell from the knots
    That held the pear to the gable-wall.
The broken sheds look'd sad and strange:
    Unlifted was the clinking latch;
    Weeded and worn the ancient thatch
Upon the lonely moated grange.
        She only said, 'My life is dreary,
          He cometh not,' she said;
        She said, 'I am aweary, aweary,
          I would that I were dead!'

Her tears fell with the dews at even;
   Her tears fell ere the dews were dried;
She could not look on the sweet heaven,
   Either at morn or eventide.
After the flitting of the bats,
   When thickest dark did trance the sky,
   She drew her casement-curtain by,
And glanced athwart the glooming flats.
     She only said, 'The night is dreary,
      He cometh not,' she said;
     She said, 'I am aweary, aweary,
      I would that I were dead!'

Upon the middle of the night,
   Waking she heard the night-fowl crow:
The cock sung out an hour ere light:
   From the dark fen the oxen's low
Came to her: without hope of change,
   In sleep she seem'd to walk forlorn,
   Till cold winds woke the gray-eyed morn
About the lonely moated grange.
     She only said, 'The day is dreary,
      He cometh not,' she said;
     She said, 'I am aweary, aweary,
      I would that I were dead!'

About a stone-cast from the wall
   A sluice with blacken'd waters slept,
And o'er it many, round and small,
   The cluster'd marish-mosses crept.
Hard by a poplar shook alway,
   All silver-green with gnarled bark:
   For leagues no other tree did mark
The level waste, the rounding gray.
     She only said, 'My life is dreary,
      He cometh not,' she said;
     She said, 'I am aweary, aweary,
      I would that I were dead!'

And ever when the moon was low,
   And the shrill winds were up and away,
In the white curtain, to and fro,
   She saw the gusty shadow sway.
But when the moon was very low,
   And wild winds bound within their cell,
   The shadow of the poplar fell
Upon her bed, across her brow.
      She only said, 'The night is dreary,
        He cometh not,' she said;
      She said, 'I am aweary, aweary,
        I would that I were dead!'

All day within the dreamy house,
   The doors upon their hinges creak'd;
The blue fly sung in the pane; the mouse
   Behind the mouldering wainscot shriek'd,
Or from the crevice peer'd about.
   Old faces glimmer'd thro' the doors,
   Old footsteps trod the upper floors,
Old voices called her from without.
      She only said, 'My life is dreary,
        He cometh not,' she said;
      She said, 'I am aweary, aweary,
        I would that I were dead!'

The sparrow's chirrup on the roof,
   The slow clock ticking, and the sound
Which to the wooing wind aloof
   The poplar made, did all confound
Her sense; but most she loathed the hour
   When the thick-moted sunbeam lay
   Athwart the chambers, and the day
Was sloping toward his western bower.
      Then, said she, 'I am very dreary,
        He will not come,' she said;
      She wept, 'I am aweary, aweary,
        Oh God, that I were dead!'

Alfred Tennyson

'THE NIGHT IS FREEZING FAST'

The night is freezing fast,
  To-morrow comes December;
    And winterfalls of old
Are with me from the past;
  And chiefly I remember
    How Dick would hate the cold.

Fall, winter, fall; for he,
  Prompt hand and headpiece clever,
    Has woven a winter robe,
And made of earth and sea
  His overcoat for ever,
    And wears the turning globe.

A.E. Housman

'I LOOK INTO MY GLASS'

I look into my glass,
And view my wasting skin,
And say, 'Would God it came to pass
My heart had shrunk as thin!'

For then, I, undistrest
By hearts grown cold to me,
Could lonely wait my endless rest
With equanimity.

But Time, to make me grieve,
Part steals, lets part abide;
And shakes this fragile frame at eve
With throbbings of noontide.

Thomas Hardy

195

Sonnet: 'WHEN TO THE SESSIONS'

When to the Sessions of sweet silent thought
I summon up remembrance of things past,
I sigh the lack of many a thing I sought,
And with old woes new wail my dear time's waste:
Then can I drown an eye, unused to flow,
For precious friends hid in death's dateless night,
And weep afresh love's long-since-cancell'd woe,
And moan th' expense of many a vanish'd sight:
Then can I grieve at grievances foregone,
And heavily from woe to woe tell o'er
The sad account of fore-bemoanèd moan,
Which I new pay as if not paid before.
    But if the while I think on thee, dear friend,
    All losses are restored and sorrows end.

William Shakespeare

'THE FORCE THAT THROUGH THE GREEN FUSE'

The force that through the green fuse drives the flower
Drives my green age; that blasts the roots of trees
Is my destroyer.
And I am dumb to tell the crooked rose
My youth is bent by the same wintry fever.

The force that drives the water through the rocks
Drives my red blood; that dries the mouthing streams
Turns mine to wax.
And I am dumb to mouth unto my veins
How at the mountain spring the same mouth sucks.

The hand that whirls the water in the pool
Stirs the quicksand; that ropes the blowing wind
Hauls my shroud sail.

And I am dumb to tell the hanging man
How of my clay is made the hangman's lime.

The lips of time leech to the fountain head;
Love drips and gathers, but the fallen blood
Shall calm her sores.
And I am dumb to tell a weather's wind
How time has ticked a heaven round the stars.

And I am dumb to tell the lover's tomb
How at my sheet goes the same crooked worm.

Dylan Thomas

AUGUST

The shutter of time darkening ceaselessly
Has whisked away the foam of may and elder
And I realise how now, as every year before,
Once again the gay months have eluded me.

For the mind, by nature stagey, welds its frame
Tomb-like around each little world of a day;
We jump from picture to picture and cannot follow
The living curve that is breathlessly the same.

While the lawn-mower sings moving up and down
Spirting its little fountain of vivid green,
I, like Poussin, make a still-bound fête of us
Suspending every noise, of insect or machine.

Garlands at a set angle that do not slip,
Theatrically (and as if for ever) grace
You and me and the stone god in the garden
And Time who also is shown with a stone face.

But all this is a dilettante's lie,
Time's face is not stone nor still his wings,
Our mind, being dead, wishes to have time die
For we being ghosts cannot catch hold of things.

Louis Macneice

THE SADNESS OF THINGS FOR SAPPHO'S
SICKNESS

Lilies will languish; violets look ill,
Sickly the primrose; pale the daffodil;
That gallant tulip will hang down his head,
Like to a virgin newly ravished;
Pansies will weep, and marigolds will wither,
And keep a fast and funeral together;
If Sappho droop, daisies will open never,
But bid good-night, and close their lids for ever.

Robert Herrick

THE GARDEN OF PROSERPINE

Here, where the world is quiet;
   Here, where all trouble seems
Dead winds' and spent waves' riot
   In doubtful dreams of dreams;
I watch the green field growing
For reaping folk and sowing,
For harvest-time and mowing,
   A sleepy world of streams.

I am tired of tears and laughter,
   And men that laugh and weep;
Of what may come hereafter
   For men that sow to reap:
I am weary of days and hours,
Blown buds of barren flowers,
Desires and dreams and powers
   And everything but sleep.

Here life has death for neighbour,
   And far from eye or ear
Wan waves and wet winds labour,
   Weak ships and spirits steer;

They drive adrift, and whither
They wot not who make thither;
But no such winds blow hither,
    And no such things grow here.

No growth of moor or coppice,
    No heather-flower or vine,
But bloomless buds of poppies,
    Green grapes of Proserpine,
Pale beds of blowing rushes
Where no leaf blooms or blushes
Save this whereout she crushes
    For dead men deadly wine.

Pale, without name or number,
    In fruitless fields of corn,
They bow themselves and slumber
    All night till light is born;
And like a soul belated,
In hell and heaven unmated,
By cloud and mist abated
    Comes out of darkness morn.

Though one were strong as seven,
    He too with death shall dwell,
Nor wake with wings in heaven,
    Nor weep for pains in hell;
Though one were fair as roses,
His beauty clouds and closes;
And well though love reposes,
    In the end it is not well.

Pale, beyond porch and portal,
    Crowned with calm leaves, she stands
Who gathers all things mortal
    With cold immortal hands;

Her languid lips are sweeter
Than love's who fears to greet her
To men that mix and meet her
    From many times and lands.

She waits for each and other,
    She waits for all men born;
Forgets the earth her mother,
    The life of fruits and corn;
And spring and seed and swallow
Take wing for her and follow
Where summer song rings hollow
    And flowers are put to scorn.

There go the loves that wither,
    The old loves with wearier wings;
And all dead years draw thither,
    And all disastrous things;
Dead dreams of days forsaken,
Blind buds that snows have shaken,
Wild leaves that winds have taken,
    Red strays of ruined springs.

We are not sure of sorrow,
    And joy was never sure;
To-day will die to-morrow;
    Time stoops to no man's lure;
And love, grown faint and fretful,
With lips but half regretful
Sighs, and with eyes forgetful
    Weeps that no loves endure.

From too much love of living,
    From hope and fear set free,
We thank with brief thanksgiving
    Whatever gods may be

That no life lives for ever;
That dead men rise up never;
That even the weariest river
   Winds somewhere safe to sea.

Then star nor sun shall waken.
   Nor any change of light:
Nor sound of waters shaken,
   Nor any sound or sight:
Nor wintry leaves nor vernal,
Nor days nor things diurnal;
Only the sleep eternal
   In an eternal night.

Algernon Charles Swinburne

SPRING AND FALL
To a Young Child

Márgarét, are you grievíng
Over Goldengrove unleaving?
Leáves, like the things of man, you
With your fresh thoughts care for, can you?
Áh! ás the heart grows older
It will come to such sights colder
By and by, nor spare a sigh
Though worlds of wanwood leafmeal lie;
And yet you will weep and know why.
Now no matter, child, the name:
Sórrow's springs áre the same.
Nor mouth had, no nor mind, expressed
What heart heard of, ghost guessed:
It ís the blight man was born for,
It is Margaret you mourn for.

Gerard Manley Hopkins

No, no! go not to Lethe, neither twist
    Wolf's-bane, tight-rooted, for its poisonous wine;
Nor suffer thy pale forehead to be kist
    By nightshade, ruby grape of Proserpine;
Make not your rosary of yew-berries,
      Nor let the beetle, nor the death-moth be
         Your mournful Psyche, nor the downy owl
A partner in your sorrow's mysteries;
      For shade to shade will come too drowsily,
         And drown the wakeful anguish of the soul.

But when the melancholy fit shall fall
    Sudden from heaven like a weeping cloud,
That fosters the droop-headed flowers all,
    And hides the green hill in an April shroud;
Then glut thy sorrow on a morning rose,
      Or on the rainbow of the salt sand-wave,
         Or on the wealth of globèd peonies;
Or if thy mistress some rich anger shows,
      Emprison her soft hand, and let her rave,
         And feed deep, deep upon her peerless eyes.

She dwells with Beauty — Beauty that must die;
    And Joy, whose hand is ever at his lips
Bidding adieu; and aching Pleasure nigh,
    Turning to Poison while the bee-mouth sips:
Ay, in the very temple of delight
      Veil'd Melancholy has her sovran shrine,
         Though seen of none save him whose strenuous tongue
Can burst Joy's grape against his palate fine;
      His soul shall taste the sadness of her might,
         And be among her cloudy trophies hung.

John Keats

THE CHERRY TREES

The cherry trees bend over and are shedding,
On the old road where all that passed are dead,
Their petals, strewing the grass as for a wedding
This early May morn when there is none to wed.

Edward Thomas

' 'TIS TIME, I THINK '

'Tis time, I think, by Wenlock town
   The golden broom should blow;
The hawthorn sprinkled up and down
   Should charge the land with snow.

Spring will not wait the loiterer's time
   Who keeps so long away;
So others wear the broom and climb
   The hedgerows heaped with may.

Oh tarnish late on Wenlock Edge,
   Gold that I never see;
Lie long, high snowdrifts in the hedge
   That will not shower on me.

A.E. Housman

SONG

A spirit haunts the year's last hours
Dwelling amid these yellowing bowers:
   To himself he talks;
For at eventide, listening earnestly,
At his work you may hear him sob and sigh
   In the walks;
   Earthward he boweth the heavy stalks
Of the mouldering flowers:

Heavily hangs the broad sunflower
Over its grave i' the earth so chilly;
Heavily hangs the hollyhock,
Heavily hangs the tiger-lily.

The air is damp, and hush'd, and close
As a sick man's room when he taketh repose
An hour before death;
My very heart faints and my whole soul grieves
At the moist rich smell of the rotting leaves,
And the breath
Of the fading edges of box beneath,
And the year's last rose.
Heavily hangs the broad sunflower
Over its grave i' the earth so chilly;
Heavily hangs the hollyhock,
Heavily hangs the tiger-lily.

Alfred Tennyson

ELEGY

The wood is bare: the river-mist is steeping
The trees that winter's chill of life bereaves:
Only their stiffened boughs break silence, weeping
Over their fallen leaves;

That lie upon the dank earth brown and rotten,
  Miry and matted in the soaking wet:
Forgotten with the spring, that is forgotten
    By them that can forget.

Yet it was here we walked when ferns were springing,
  And through the mossy bank shot bud and blade: —
Here found in summer, when the birds were singing,
    A green and pleasant shade.

'Twas here we loved in sunnier days and greener;
  And now, in this disconsolate decay,
I come to see her where I most have seen her,
    And touch the happier day.

For on this path, at every turn and corner,
  The fancy of her figure on me falls:
Yet walks she with the slow step of a mourner,
    Nor hears my voice that calls.

So through my heart there winds a track of feeling,
  A path of memory, that is all her own:
Whereto her phantom beauty ever stealing
    Haunts the sad spot alone.

About her steps the trunks are bare, the branches
  Drip heavy tears upon her downcast head;
And bleed from unseen wounds that no sun stanches,
    For the year's sun is dead.

And dead leaves wrap the fruits that summer planted:
  And birds that love the South have taken wing.
The wanderer, loitering o'er the scene enchanted,
  Weeps, and despairs of spring.

                              Robert Bridges

A COMMONPLACE DAY

The day is turning ghost,
And scuttles from the kalendar in fits and furtively,
To join the anonymous host
Of those that throng oblivion; ceding his place, maybe,
To one of like degree.

I part the fire-gnawed logs,
Rake forth the embers, spoil the busy flames, and lay the
    ends
Upon the shining dogs;
Further and further from the nooks the twilight's stride
    extends,
And beamless black impends.

Nothing of tiniest worth
Have I wrought, pondered, planned; no one thing asking
    blame or praise,
Since the pale corpse-like birth
Of this diurnal unit, bearing blanks in all its rays —
Dullest of dull-hued Days!

Wanly upon the panes
The rain slides, as have slid since morn my colourless
    thoughts; and yet
Here, while Day's presence wanes,
And over him the sepulchre-lid is slowly lowered and set,
He wakens my regret.

Regret — though nothing dear
That I wot of, was toward in the wide world at his prime,
Or bloomed elsewhere than here,
To die with his decease, and leave a memory sweet, sublime,
Or mark him out in Time. . .

— Yet, maybe, in some soul,
In some spot undiscerned on sea or land, some impulse rose,
Or some intent upstole

Of that enkindling ardency from whose maturer glows
    The world's amendment flows;

    But which, benumbed at birth
By momentary chance or wile, has missed its hope to be
    Embodied on the earth;
And undervoicings of this loss to man's futurity
    May wake regret in me.

Thomas Hardy

THE OWL

Downhill I came, hungry, and yet not starved;
Cold, yet had heat within me that was proof
Against the North wind; tired, yet so that rest
Had seemed the sweetest thing under a roof.

Then at the inn I had food, fire, and rest,
Knowing how hungry, cold, and tired was I.
All of the night was quite barred out except
An owl's cry, a most melancholy cry

Shaken out long and clear upon the hill,
No merry note, nor cause of merriment,
But one telling me plain what I escaped
And others could not, that night, as in I went.

And salted was my food, and my repose,
Salted and sobered, too, by the bird's voice
Speaking for all who lay under the stars,
Soldiers and poor, unable to rejoice.

Edward Thomas

HIS IMMORTALITY

I saw a dead man's finer part
Shining within each faithful heart
Of those bereft. Then said I: 'This must be
    His immortality.'

I looked there as the seasons wore,
And still his soul continuously bore
A life in theirs. But less its shine excelled
    Than when I first beheld.

His fellow-yearsmen passed, and then
In later hearts I looked for him again;
And found him — shrunk, alas! into a thin
    And spectral mannikin.

Lastly I ask — now old and chill —
If aught of him remain unperished still;
And find, in me alone, a feeble spark,
    Dying amid the dark.

Thomas Hardy

IN A DREAR-NIGHTED DECEMBER

In a drear-nighted December,
Too happy, happy tree,
Thy branches ne'er remember
Their green felicity:
The north cannot undo them
With a sleety whistle through them;
Nor frozen thawings glue them
From budding at the prime.

In a drear-nighted December,
Too happy, happy brook,
Thy bubblings ne'er remember
Apollo's summer look;
But with a sweet forgetting,
They stay their crystal fretting,
Never, never petting
About the frozen time.

Ah! would 'twere so with many
A gentle girl and boy!
But were there ever any
Writhed not at passèd joy?
To know the change and feel it,
When there is none to heal it,
Nor numbed sense to steal it,
Was never said in rhyme.

John Keats

Sonnet 'THAT TIME OF YEAR'

That time of year thou may'st in me behold
When yellow leaves, or none, or few, do hang
Upon those boughs which shake against the cold —
Bare ruin'd choirs where late the sweet birds sang.
In me thou see'st the twilight of such day
As after sunset fadeth in the West,
Which by and by black night doth take away,
Death's second self, that seals up all in rest.
In me thou see'st the glowing of such fire
That on the ashes of his youth doth lie,
As the death-bed whereon it must expire,
Consumed with that which it was nourish'd by.
    This thou perceiv'st, which makes thy love more strong
    To love that well which thou must leave ere long.

William Shakespeare

ON HIS DECEASED WIFE

Methought I saw my late espoused Saint
 Brought to me like Alcestis from the grave,
 Whom Jove's great Son to her glad Husband gave,
 Rescu'd from death by force though pale and faint.
Mine as whom washt from spot of child-bed taint,
 Purification in the old Law did save,
 And such, as yet once more I trust to have
 Full sight of her in Heaven without restraint,
Came vested all in white, pure as her mind:
 Her face was vail'd, yet to my fancied sight,
 Love, sweetness, goodness, in her person shin'd
So clear, as in no face with more delight.
 But O as to embrace me she enclin'd
 I wak'd, she fled, and day brought back my night.

John Milton

SURPRISED BY JOY

Surprised by joy — impatient as the Wind
 I turned to share the transport — O! with whom
 But Thee, deep buried in the silent tomb,
That spot which no vicissitude can find?
Love, faithful love, recall'd thee to my mind —
 But how could I forget thee? Through what power,
 Even for the least division of an hour,
Have I been so beguiled as to be blind
To my most grievous loss? — That thought's return
 Was the worst pang that sorrow ever bore,
Save one, one only, when I stood forlorn,
 Knowing my heart's best treasure was no more;
That neither present time, nor years unborn
 Could to my sight that heavenly face restore.

William Wordsworth

Sonnet: 'I WAKE AND FEEL THE FELL OF DARK'

I wake and feel the fell of dark, not day.
What hours, O what black hoürs we have spent
This night! what sights you, heart, saw; ways you went!
And more must, in yet longer light's delay.
⠀⠀⠀With witness I speak this. But where I say
Hours I mean years, mean life. And my lament
Is cries countless, cries like dead letters sent
To dearest him that lives alas! away,

⠀⠀⠀I am gall, I am heartburn. God's most deep decree
Bitter would have me taste: my taste was me;
Bones built in me, flesh filled, blood brimmed the curse.
⠀⠀⠀Selfyeast of spirit a dull dough sours. I see
The lost are like this, and their scourge to be
As I am mine, their sweating selves; but worse.

⠀⠀⠀⠀⠀⠀⠀⠀⠀⠀⠀⠀⠀⠀⠀⠀*Gerard Manley Hopkins*

AFTERWARDS

When the Present has latched its postern behind my
⠀⠀⠀tremulous stay,
⠀⠀And the May month flaps its glad green leaves like wings,
Delicate-filmed as new-spun silk, will the neighbours say,
⠀⠀'He was a man who used to notice such things'?

If it be in the dusk when, like an eyelid's soundless blink,
⠀⠀The dewfall-hawk comes crossing the shades to alight
Upon the wind-warped upland thorn, a gazer may think,
⠀⠀'To him this must have been a familiar sight.'

If I pass during some nocturnal blackness, mothy and warm,
⠀⠀When the hedgehog travels furtively over the lawn,
One may say,'He strove that such innocent creatures should
⠀⠀⠀come to no harm,
⠀⠀But he could do little for them; and now he is gone.'

⠀⠀⠀⠀⠀⠀⠀⠀⠀⠀⠀⠀⠀⠀⠀⠀211

If, when hearing that I have been stilled at last, they
    stand at the door,
  Watching the full-starred heavens that winter sees,
Will this thought rise on those who will meet my face no
    more,
  'He was one who had an eye for such mysteries'?

And will any say when my bell of quittance is heard in the
    gloom,
  And a crossing breeze cuts a pause in its outrollings,
Till they rise again, as they were a new bell's boom,
  'He hears it not now, but used to notice such things'?

Thomas Hardy

DOVER BEACH

The sea is calm to-night,
The tide is full, the moon lies fair
Upon the Straits; — on the French coast, the light
Gleams, and is gone; the cliffs of England stand,
Glimmering and vast, out in the tranquil bay.
Come to the window, sweet is the night air!
Only, from the long line of spray
Where the ebb meets the moon-blanch'd sand,
Listen! you hear the grating roar
Of pebbles which the waves suck back, and fling,
At their return, up the high strand,
Begin, and cease, and then again begin,
With tremulous cadence slow, and bring
The eternal note of sadness in.

Sophocles long ago
Heard it on the Ægaen, and it brought
Into his mind the turbid ebb and flow
Of human misery; we
Find also in the sound a thought,
Hearing it by this distant northern sea.

The sea of faith
Was once, too, at the full, and round earth's shore
Lay like the folds of a bright girdle furl'd;
But now I only hear
Its melancholy, long, withdrawing roar,
Retreating to the breath
Of the night-wind down the vast edges drear
And naked shingles of the world.

Ah, love, let us be true
To one another! for the world, which seems
To lie before us like a land of dreams,
So various, so beautiful, so new,
Hath really neither joy, nor love, nor light,
Nor certitude, nor peace, nor help for pain;
And we are here as on a darkling plain
Swept with confused alarms of struggle and flight,
Where ignorant armies clash by night.

Matthew Arnold

MANY A LONG YEAR

Says the auld man
To the oak tree,
'Young and lusty was I
When I kenned thee.

'I was young and lusty,
I was fair and clear,
Young and lusty was I
Many a long year.

'But sair failed am I,
Sair failed noo,
Sair failed am I
Sin I kenned you.'

Anon.

213

10

NIGHT, MOON AND STARS

The moon shines bright
The stars give a light;
We'll see to kiss a pretty lass
At ten oclock at night

ANON

IN THE DARK NONE DAINTY

Night hides our thefts, all faults then pardon'd be;
All are alike fair when no spots we see.
Lais and Lucrece in the night-time are
Pleasing alike, alike both singular:
Joan and my lady have at that time one,
One and the self-same pris'd complexion:
Then please alike the pewter and the plate,
The chosen ruby, and the reprobate.

Robert Herrick

DREAM-SONG

Sunlight, moonlight,
Twilight, starlight —
Gloaming at the close of day,
And an owl calling,
Cool dews falling
In a wood of oak and may.

Lantern-light, taper-light,
Torchlight, no-light:
Darkness at the shut of day,
And lions roaring,
Their wrath pouring
In wild waste places far away.

Elf-light, bat-light,
Touchwood-light and toad-light,
And the sea a shimmering gloom of grey,
And a small face smiling
In a dream's beguiling
In a world of wonders far away.

Walter de la Mare

TO-NIGHT

Harry, you know at night
The larks in Castle Alley
Sing from the attic's height
As if the electric light
Were the true sun above a summer valley:
Whistle, don't knock, to-night.

I shall come early, Kate:
And we in Castle Alley
Will sit close out of sight
Alone, and ask no light
Of lamp or sun above a summer valley:
To-night I can stay late.

Edward Thomas

THE NIGHT-PIECE: TO JULIA

Her eyes the glow-worm lend thee,
The shooting stars attend thee;
    And the elves also,
    Whose little eyes glow
Like the sparks of fire, befriend thee.

No Will-o'-the-wisp mislight thee,
Nor snake or slow-worm bite thee;
    But on, on thy way
    Not making a stay,
Since ghost there's none to affright thee.

Let not the dark thee cumber:
What though the moon does slumber?
   The stars of the night
   Will lend thee their light
Like tapers clear without number.

Then, Julia, let me woo thee,
Thus, thus to come unto me;
   And when I shall meet
   Thy silv'ry feet
My soul I'll pour into thee.

Robert Herrick

'US IDLE WENCHES'

It was a jolly bed in sooth,
   Of oak as strong as Babel.
And there slept Kit and Sall and Ruth
   As sound as maids are able.

Ay — three in one — and there they dreamed,
   Their bright young eyes hid under;
Nor hearkened when the tempest streamed
   Nor recked the rumbling thunder.

For marvellous regions strayed they in,
   Each moon — far from the other —
Ruth in her childhood, Kit in heaven,
   And Sall with ghost for lover.

But soon as ever sun shone sweet,
   And birds sang Praise for rain, O —
Leapt out of bed three pair of feet
   And danced on earth again, O!

Anon.

Eddi, priest of St. Wilfrid
   In the chapel at Manhood End,
Ordered a midnight service
   For such as cared to attend.

But the Saxons were keeping Christmas,
   And the night was stormy as well.
Nobody came to service
   Though Eddi rang the bell.

'Wicked weather for walking,'
   Said Eddi of Manhood End.
'But I must go on with the service
   For such as care to attend.'

The altar candles were lighted, —
   An old marsh donkey came,
Bold as a guest invited,
   And stared at the guttering flame.

The storm beat on at the windows,
   The water splashed on the floor,
And a wet yoke-weary bullock
   Pushed in through the open door.

'How do I know what is greatest,
   How do I know what is least?
That is My Father's business.'
   Said Eddi, Wilfrid's priest.

'But, three are gathered together —
   Listen to me and attend.
I bring good news, my brethren!'
   Said Eddi, of Manhood End.

And he told the Ox of a manger
  And a stall in Bethlehem,
And he spoke to the Ass of a Rider
  That rode to Jerusalem.

They steamed and dripped in the chancel,
  They listened and never stirred,
While, just as though they were Bishops,
  Eddi preached them The Word.

Till the gale blew off on the marshes
  And the windows showed the day,
And the Ox and the Ass together
  Wheeled and clattered away.

And when the Saxons mocked him,
  Said Eddi of Manhood End,
'I dare not shut His chapel
  On such as care to attend.'

Rudyard Kipling

From THE MERCHANT OF VENICE

Lorenzo. The moon shines bright. In such a night as this,
When the sweet wind did gently kiss the trees,
And they did make no noise, in such a night
Troilus methinks mounted the Troyan walls,
And sighed his soul toward the Grecian tents,
Where Cressid lay that night.
Jessica. In such a night
Did Thisbe fearfully o'ertrip the dew,
And saw the lion's shadow ere himself,
And ran dismayed away.
Lorenzo. In such a night
Stood Dido with a willow in her hand
Upon the wild sea banks, and waft her love
To come again to Carthage . . . .

How sweet the moonlight sleeps upon this bank!
Here will we sit and let the sounds of music
Creep in our ears — soft stillness and the night
Become the touches of sweet harmony.
Sit, Jessica. Look how the floor of heaven
Is thick inlaid with patens of bright gold.
There's not the smallest orb which thou behold'st
But in his motion like an angel sings,
Still choiring to the young-eyed cherubins . . . .

William Shakespeare

220

HYMN TO DIANA

Queen and huntress, chaste and fair,
  Now the sun is laid to sleep,
Seated in thy silver chair,
    State in wonted manner keep:
      Hesperus entreats thy light,
      Goddess excellently bright.

Earth, let not thy envious shade
  Dare itself to interpose;
Cynthia's shining orb was made
    Heaven to clear when day did close:
      Bless us then with wishèd sight,
      Goddess excellently bright.

Lay thy bow of pearl apart,
  And thy crystal-shining quiver;
Give unto the flying hart
    Space to breathe, how short soever:
      Thou that mak'st a day of night —
      Goddess excellently bright.

Ben Jonson

ELIZABETH OF BOHEMIA

You meaner beauties of the night,
  That poorly satisfy our eyes
More by your number than your light,
  You common people of the skies;
    What are you when the moon shall rise?

You curious chanters of the wood,
    That warble forth Dame Nature's lays,
Thinking your passions understood
    By your weak accents; what's your praise
    When Philomel her voice shall raise?

You violets that first appear,
    By your pure purple mantles known
Like the proud virgins of the year,
    As if the spring were all your own;
    What are you when the rose is blown?

So, when my mistress shall be seen
    In form and beauty of her mind,
By virtue first, then choice, a Queen,
    Tell me, if she were not designed
    The eclipse and glory of her kind?

                                Sir Henry Wotton

THE STARLIGHT NIGHT

Look at the stars! look, look up at the skies!
    O look at all the fire-folk sitting in the air!
    The bright boroughs, the circle-citadels there!
Down in dim woods the diamond delves! the elves'-eyes!
The grey lawns cold where gold, where quickgold lies!
    Wind-beat whitebeam! airy abeles set on a flare!
    Flake-doves sent floating forth at a farmyard scare! —
Ah well! it is all a purchase, all is a prize.

Buy then! bid then! — What? — Prayer, patience, alms, vows.
Look, look: a May-mess, like on orchard boughs!
    Look! March-bloom, like on mealed-with-yellow sallows!
These are indeed the barn; withindoors house
The shocks. This piece-bright paling shuts the spouse
    Christ home, Christ and his mother and all his hallows.

                                Gerard Manley Hopkins

222

THE MOWER TO THE GLOW-WORMS

Ye living lamps, by whose dear light
The nightingale does sit so late,
And studying all the summer night,
Her matchless songs does meditate;

Ye country comets, that portend
No war nor prince's funeral,
Shining unto no higher end
Than to presage the grass's fall;

Ye glow-worms, whose officious flame
To wandering mowers shows the way,
That in the night have lost their aim,
And after foolish fires do stray;

Your courteous lights in vain you waste,
Since Juliana here is come,
For she my mind hath so displaced,
That I shall never find my home.

Andrew Marvell

OLD SHELLOVER

'Come!' said Old Shellover.
'What?' says Creep.
'The horny old Gardener's fast asleep;
The fat cock Thrush
To his nest has gone;

And the dew shines bright
In the rising Moon;
Old Sallie Worm from her hole doth peep:
Come!' said Old Shellover.
'Ay!' said Creep.

Walter de la Mare

A WATER-PARTY

Let us, as by this verdant bank we float,
Search down the marge to find some shady pool
Where we may rest awhile and moor our boat,
And bathe our tired limbs in the waters cool.
   Beneath the noonday sun,
   Swiftly, O river, run!

Here is a mirror for Narcissus, see!
I cannot sound it, plumbing with my oar.
Lay the stern in beneath this bowering tree!
Now, stepping on this stump, we are ashore.
   Guard, Hamadryades,
   Our clothes laid by your trees!

How the birds warble in the woods! I pick
The waxen lilies, diving to the root.
But swim not far in the stream, the weeds grow thick,
And hot on the bare head the sunbeams shoot.
   Until our sport be done,
   O merry birds, sing on!

If but to-night the sky be clear, the moon
Will serve us well, for she is near the full.
We shall row safely home; only too soon, —
So pleasant 'tis, whether we float or pull.
   To guide us through the night,
   O summer moon, shine bright!

Robert Bridges

FROM 'THYRSIS'

So, some tempestuous morn in early June,
When the year's primal burst of bloom is o'er,
Before the roses and the longest day —
When garden-walks, and all the grassy floor,
With blossoms, red and white, of fallen May,
And chestnut-flowers are strewn —
So have I heard the cuckoo's parting cry,
From the wet field, through the vext garden-trees,
Come with the volleying rain and tossing breeze:
The bloom is gone, and with the bloom go I.

Too quick despairer, wherefore wilt thou go?
Soon will the high Midsummer pomps come on,
Soon will the musk carnations break and swell,
Soon shall we have gold-dusted snapdragon,
Sweet-William with its homely cottage-smell,
And stocks in fragrant blow;
Roses that down the alleys shine afar,
And open, jasmine-muffled lattices,
And groups under the dreaming garden-trees,
And the full moon, and the white evening-star.

Matthew Arnold

A NOCTURNAL UPON ST. LUCY'S DAY

'Tis the year's midnight, and it is the day's,
Lucy's, who scarce seven hours herself unmasks;
   The Sun is spent, and now his flasks
   Send forth light squibs, no constant rays;
     The world's whole sap is sunk
The general balm th'hydroptic earth hath drunk,
Whither, as to the bed's feet, life is shrunk,
Dead and interr'd; yet all these seem to laugh,
Compar'd with me, who am their Epitaph.

Study me then, you who shall lovers be
At the next world, that is, at the next Spring:
For I am every dead thing,
In whom love wrought new alchemy.
For his art did express
A quintessence even from nothingness,
From dull privations, and lean emptiness:
He ruin'd me, and I am re-begot
Of absense, darkness, death; things which are not.

All others, from all things, draw all that's good,
Life, soul, form, spirit, whence they being have
I, by love's limbec, am the grave
Of all, that's nothing. Oft a flood
Have we two wept, and so
Drown'd the whole world, us two; oft did we grow
To be two Chaoses, when we did show
Care to aught else; and often absences
Withdrew our souls, and made us carcases.

But I am by her death (which word wrongs her)
Of the first nothing, the Elixir grown;
Were I a man, that I were one,
I needs must know; I should prefer,
If I were any beast,
Some ends, some means; yea plants, yea stones detest,
And love; all, all some properties invest;
If I an ordinary nothing were,
As shadow, a light, and body must be here.

But I am None; nor will my Sun renew.
You lovers, for whose sake, the lesser Sun
At this time to the Goat is run
To fetch new lusts and give it you,
Enjoy your summer all;
Since she enjoys her long night's festival,
Let me prepare towards her, and let me call
This hour her Vigil, and her Eve, since this
Both the year's, and the day's deep midnight is.

John Donne

THE WANING MOON

And like a dying lady, lean and pale,
Who totters forth, wrapped in a gauzy veil,
Out of her chamber, led by the insane
And feeble wanderings of her fading brain,
The moon arose up in the murky East,
A white and shapeless mass —

Percy Bysshe Shelley

OUT IN THE DARK

Out in the dark over the snow
The fallow fawns invisible go
With the fallow doe;
And the winds blow
Fast as the stars are slow.

Stealthily the dark haunts round
And, when the lamp goes, without sound
At a swifter bound
Than the swiftest hound,
Arrives, and all else is drowned;

And I and star and wind and deer,
Are in the dark together, — near,
Yet far, — and fear
Drums on my ear
In that sage company drear.

How weak and little is the light,
All the universe of sight,
Love and delight,
Before the might,
If you love it not, of night.

Edward Thomas

THE BELL-MAN

From noise of Scare-fires rest ye free,
From Murders — Benedicite.
From all mischances, that may fright
Your pleasing slumbers in the night:
Mercy secure ye all, and keep
The Goblin from ye, while ye sleep.
Past one o'clock, and almost two,
My Masters all, Good day to you!

Robert Herrick

MERLIN'S ISLE OF GRAMARYE

. . . The same that oft-times hath
Charm'd magic casements, opening on the foam
Of perilous seas, in faery lands forlorn

KEATS

THE FAIRY QUEEN

Come follow, follow me,
You, fairy elves that be:
Which circle on the greene,
Come follow Mab your queene.
Hand in hand let's dance around,
For this place is fairye ground.

When mortals are at rest,
And snoring in their nest;
Unheard, and unespy'd,
Through key-holes we do glide;
Over tables, stools, and shelves,
We trip it with our fairy elves.

And, if the house be foul
With platter, dish, or bowl,
Upstairs we nimbly creep,
And find the sluts asleep;
There we pinch their armes and thighes;
None escapes, nor none espies.

But if the house be swept,
And from uncleanness kept,
We praise the household maid,
And duely she is paid:
For we use before we goe
To drop a tester in her shoe.

Upon a mushroome's head
Our table-cloth we spread;
A grain of rye, or wheat,
Is manchet, which we eat;
Pearly drops of dew we drink
In acorn cups fill'd to the brink.

The brains of nightingales,
With unctuous fat of snailes,
Between two cockles stew'd,
Is meat that's easily chew'd;
Tailes of wormes, and marrow of mice,
Do make a dish that's wondrous nice.

The grasshopper, gnat, and fly,
Serve for our minstrelsie;
Grace said, we dance a while,
And so the time beguile:
And if the moon doth hide her head,
The gloe-worm lights us home to bed.

On tops of dewie grasse
So nimbly do we passe;
The young and tender stalk
Ne'er bends when we do walk:
Yet in the morning may be seen
Where we the night before have been.

Anon.

FAREWELL, REWARDS AND FAIRIES

'Farewell, rewards and fairies!'
    Good housewives now may say,
For now foul sluts in dairies
    Do fare as well as they.
And though they sweep their hearths no less
    Than maids were wont to do,
Yet who of late, for cleanliness,
    Finds sixpence in her shoe? . . . .

At morning and at evening both
    You merry were and glad;
So little care of sleep or sloth
    These pretty ladies had;
When Tom came home from labour,
    Or Ciss to milking rose,
Then merrily merrily went their tabour
    And nimbly went their toes.

Witness those rings and roundelays
    Of theirs, which yet remain,
Were footed in Queen Mary's days
    On many a grassy plain;
But since of late, Elizabeth,
    And later, James came in,
They never danced on any heath
    As when the time hath been.

Bishop Corbett

From A MIDSUMMER-NIGHT'S DREAM

Oberon: I know a bank where the wild thyme blows,
Where oxlips and the nodding violet grows,
Quite over-canopied with luscious woodbine,
With sweet musk-roses, and with eglantine:
There sleeps Titania sometime of the night,
Lulled in these flowers with dances and delight;
And there the snake throws her enamelled skin,
Weed wide enough to wrap a fairy in.

William Shakespeare

THE FAIRIES

Up the airy mountain,
    Down the rushy glen,
We daren't go a-hunting
    For fear of little men;
Wee folk, good folk,
    Trooping all together;
Green jacket, red cap,
    And white owl's feather!

Down along the rocky shore
    Some make their home,
They live on crispy pancakes
    Of yellow tide-foam;
Some in the reeds
    Of the black mountain lake,
With frogs for their watch-dogs,
    All night awake.

High on the hill-top
    The old King sits;
He is now so old and gray
    He's nigh lost his wits.
With a bridge of white mist
    Columbkill he crosses,
On his stately journeys
    From Slieveleague to Rosses;
Or going up with music
    On cold starry nights
To sup with the Queen
    Of the gay Northern Lights.

They stole little Bridget
    For seven years long;
When she came down again
    Her friends were all gone.

They took her lightly back,
   Between the night and morrow,
They thought that she was fast asleep,
   But she was dead with sorrow.
They have kept her ever since
   Deep within the lake,
On a bed of flag-leaves,
   Watching till she wake.

By the craggy hill-side,
   Through the mosses bare,
They have planted thorn-trees
   For pleasure here and there.
If any man so daring
   As dig them up in spite,
He shall find their sharpest thorns
   In his bed at night.

Up the airy mountain,
   Down the rushy glen,
We daren't go a-hunting
   For fear of little men;
Wee folk, good folk,
   Trooping all together;
Green jacket, red cap,
   And white owl's feather!

William Allingham

SONG FOR THE LUTE

Thrice toss these oaken ashes in the air;
Thrice sit thou mute in this enchanted chair;
Then thrice three times tie up this true love's knot,
And murmur soft: 'She will, or she will not.'

Go burn these poisonous weeds in yon blue fire,
These screech-owl's feathers and this prickling briar,

This cypress gathered at a dead man's grave,
That all thy fears and cares an end may have.

Then come, you fairies, dance with me a round;
Melt her hard heart with your melodious sound.
In vain are all the charms I can devise;
She hath an art to break them with her eyes.

Thomas Campion

'OVER HILL OVER DALE'

Over hill, over dale,
  Thorough bush, thorough briar,
Over park, over pale,
  Thorough flood, thorough fire,
  I do wander everywhere,
  Swifter than the moone's sphere;
  And I serve the fair queen,
  To dew her orbs upon the green:
  The cowslips tall her pensioners be;
  In their gold coats spots you see;
  These be rubies, fairy favours,
  In those freckles live their savours:
I must go seek some dew-drops here,
And hang a pearl in every cowslip's ear.

William Shakespeare

THE MAN WHO DREAMED OF FAERYLAND

He stood among a crowd at Drumahair;
His heart hung all upon a silken dress,
And he had known at last some tenderness,
Before earth took him to her stony care;

235

But when a man poured fish into a pile,
It seemed they raised their little silver heads,
And sang what gold morning or evening sheds
Upon a woven world-forgotten isle
Where people love beside the ravelled seas;
That Time can never mar a lover's vows
Under that woven changeless roof of boughs:
The singing shook him out of his new ease.

He wandered by the sands of Lissadell;
His mind ran all on money cares and fears,
And he had known at last some prudent years
Before they heaped his grave under the hill;
But while he passed before a plashy place,
A lug-worm with its grey and muddy mouth
Sang that somewhere to north or west or south
There dwelt a gay, exulting, gentle race
Under the golden or the silver skies;
That if a dancer stayed his hungry foot
It seemed the sun and moon were in the fruit:
And at that singing he was no more wise.

He mused beside the well of Scanavin,
He mused upon his mockers: without fail
His sudden vengeance were a country tale,
When earthy night had drunk his body in;
But one small knot-grass growing by the pool
Sang where — unnecessary cruel voice —
Old silence bids its chosen race rejoice,
Whatever ravelled waters rise and fall
Or stormy silver fret the gold of day,
And midnight there enfold them like a fleece
And lover there by lover be at peace.
The tale drove his fine angry mood away.

He slept under the hill of Lugnagall;
And might have known at last unhaunted sleep
Under that cold and vapour-turbaned steep,

Now that the earth had taken man and all:
Did not the worms that spired about his bones
Proclaim with that unwearied, reedy cry
That God has laid His fingers on the sky,
That from those fingers glittering summer runs
Upon the dancer by the dreamless wave.
Why should those lovers that no lovers miss
Dream, until God burn Nature with a kiss?
The man has found no comfort in the grave.

William Butler Yeats

I SAW A PEACOCK

I saw a peacock with a fiery tail,
I saw a blazing comet pour down hail,
I saw a cloud wrapt with ivy round.
I saw an oak creeping on the ground,
I saw a pismire swallow up a whale,
I saw the sea brimful of ale,
I saw a Venice glass fifteen feet deep,
I saw a well full of men's tears that weep,
I saw wet eyes all of a flaming fire,
I saw a horse bigger than the moon and higher,
I saw the sun even at midnight –
I saw the man who saw this dreadful sight.

Anon.

SONG

Go and catch a falling star,
   Get with child a mandrake root,
Tell me where all past years are,
   Or who cleft the Devil's foot;
Teach me to hear mermaids singing,
Or to keep off envy's stinging,
     And find
     What wind
Serves to advance an honest mind.

If thou be'st born to strange sights,
   Things invisible to see,
Ride ten thousand days and nights
   Till Age snow white hairs on thee;
Thou, when thou return'st, wilt tell me
All strange wonders that befell thee,
     And swear
     No where
Lives a woman true and fair.

If thou find'st one, let me know;
   Such a pilgrimage were sweet.
Yet do not; I would not go,
   Though at next door we might meet.
Though she were true when you met her,
And last till you write your letter,
     Yet she
     Will be
False, ere I come, to two or three.

                 John Donne

THE BUGLE

The spendour falls on castle walls
  And snowy summits old in story:
The long light shakes across the lakes,
  And the wild cataract leaps in glory.
Blow, bugle, blow, set the wild echoes flying,
Blow, bugle; answer, echoes, dying, dying, dying.

O hark, O hear! how thin and clear,
  And thinner, clearer, farther going!
O sweet and far from cliff and scar
  The horns of Elfland faintly blowing!
Blow, let us hear the purple glens replying:
Blow, bugle; answer, echoes, dying, dying, dying.

O love, they die in yon rich sky,
  They faint on hill or field or river:
Our echoes roll from soul to soul,
  And grow for ever and for ever.
Blow, bugle, blow, set the wild echoes flying,
And answer, echoes, answer, dying, dying, dying.

Alfred Tennyson

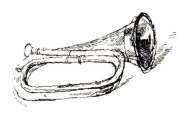

JOHN MOULDY

I spied John Mouldy in his cellar,
  Deep down twenty steps of stone;
In the dusk he sat a-smiling,
  Smiling there alone.

He read no book, he snuffed no candle;
The rats ran in, the rats ran out;
And far and near, the drip of water
    Went whisp'ring about.

The dusk was still, with dew a-falling,
I saw the Dog-star bleak and grim,
I saw a slim brown rat of Norway
    Creep over him.

I spied John Mouldy in his cellar,
Deep down twenty steps of stone;
In the dusk he sat a-smiling,
    Smiling there alone.

Walter de la Mare

THE WAY THROUGH THE WOODS

They shut the road through the woods
    Seventy years ago.
Weather and rain have undone it again,
And now you would never know
There was once a road through the woods
Before they planted the trees.
It is underneath the coppice and heath
And the thin anemones.
Only the keeper sees
That, where the ring-dove broods,
And the badgers roll at ease,
There was once a road through the woods.

Yet, if you enter the woods
Of a summer evening late,
When the night-air cools on the trout-ringed pools
Where the otter whistles his mate,
(They fear not men in the woods,
Because they see so few.)

You will hear the beat of a horse's feet,
And the swish of a skirt in the dew,
Steadily cantering through
The misty solitudes,
As though they perfectly knew
The old lost road through the woods. . .
But there is no road through the woods.

Rudyard Kipling

'WHO'S IN THE NEXT ROOM?'

'Who's in the next room? — who?
 I seemed to see
Somebody in the dawning passing through,
 Unknown to me.'
'Nay: you saw nought. He passed invisibly.'

'Who's in the next room? — who?
 I seem to hear
Somebody muttering firm in a language new
 That chills the ear.'
'No: you catch not his tongue who has entered there.'

'Who's in the next room? — who?
 I seem to feel
His breath like a clammy draught, as if it drew
 From the Polar Wheel.'
'No: none who breathes at all does the door conceal.'

'Who's in the next room? — who?
 A figure wan
With a message to one in there of something due?
 Shall I know him anon?'
'Yea he; and he brought such; and you'll know him anon.'

Thomas Hardy

THE HAUNTER

He does not think that I haunt here nightly:
    How shall I let him know
That whither his fancy sets him wandering
    I, too, alertly go?—
Hover and hover a few feet from him
    Just as I used to do,
But cannot answer the words he lifts me —
    Only listen thereto!

When I could answer he did not say them:
    When I could let him know
How I would like to join in his journeys
    Seldom he wished to go.
Now that he goes and wants me with him
    More than he used to do,
Never he sees my faithful phantom
    Though he speaks thereto.

Yes, I companion him to places
    Only dreamers know,
Where the shy hares print long paces,
    Where the night rooks go;
Into old aisles where the past is all to him,
    Close as his shade can do,
Always lacking the power to call to him,
    Near as I reach thereto!

What a good haunter I am, O tell him!
    Quickly make him know
If he but sigh since my loss befell him
    Straight to his side I go.
Tell him a faithful one is doing
    All that love can do
Still that his path may be worth pursuing,
    And to bring peace thereto.

Thomas Hardy

LA BELLE DAME SANS MERCI

O, what can ail thee, knight-at-arms,
    Alone and palely loitering;
The sedge is wither'd from the lake,
    And no birds sing.

O, what can ail thee, knight-at-arms,
    So haggard and so woe-begone?
The squirrel's granary is full,
    And the harvest's done.

I see a lily on thy brow,
    With anguish moist and fever dew;
And on thy cheek a fading rose
    Fast withereth too.

I met a lady in the meads,
    Full beautiful — a faery's child,
Her hair was long, her foot was light,
    And her eyes were wild.

I made a garland for her head,
    And bracelets too, and fragrant zone;
She look'd at me as she did love,
    And made sweet moan.

I set her on my pacing steed
    And nothing else saw all day long,
For sideways would she lean, and sing
    A faery's song.

She found me roots of relish sweet,
    And honey wild, and manna dew;
And sure in language strange she said,
    I love thee true.

She took me to her elfin grot,
    And there she wept and sigh'd full sore;
And there I shut her wild, wild eyes
    With kisses four.

And there we slumber'd on the moss,
    And there I dream'd — Ah! woe betide!
The latest dream I ever dream'd
    On the cold hill side.

I saw pale kings, and princes too,
    Pale warriors, death-pale were they all;
Who cried — 'La belle Dame sans Merci
    Hath thee in thrall!'

I saw their starv'd lips in the gloam
    With horrid warning gapèd wide,
And I awoke, and found me here
    On the cold hill side.

And this is why I sojourn here
    Alone and palely loitering,
Though the sedge is wither'd from the lake,
    And no birds sing.

John Keats

THE BALLAD OF MINEPIT SHAW

About the time that taverns shut
    And men can buy no beer,
Two lads went up by the keepers' hut
    To steal Lord Pelham's deer.

Night and the liquor was in their heads —
    They laughed and talked no bounds,
Till they waked the keepers on their beds,
    And the keepers loosed the hounds.

They had killed a hart, they had killed a hind,
    Ready to carry away,
When they heard a whimper down the wind
    And they heard a bloodhound bay.

They took and ran across the fern,
    Their crossbows in their hand,
Till they met a man with a green lantern
    That called and bade 'em stand.

'What are ye doing, O Flesh and Blood,
    And what's your foolish will,
That you must break into Minepit Wood
    And wake the Folk of the Hill?'

'Oh, we've broke into Lord Pelham's park,
    And killed Lord Pelham's deer,
And if ever you heard a little dog bark
    You'll know why we come here!

'We ask you let us go our way,
    As fast as we can flee,
For if ever you heard a bloodhound bay,
    You'll know how pressed we be.'

'Oh, lay your crossbows on the bank
    And drop the knife from your hand,
And though the hounds are at your flank
    I'll save you where you stand!'

They laid their crossbows on the bank
    They threw their knives in the wood,
And the ground before them opened and sank
    And saved 'em where they stood.

'Oh, what's the roaring in our ears
    That strikes us well-nigh dumb?'
'Oh, that is just how things appears
    According as they come.'

'What are the stars before our eyes
    That strike us well-nigh blind?'
'Oh, that is just how things arise
    According as you find.'

'And why's our bed so hard to the bones
      Excepting where it's cold?'
'Oh, that's because it is precious stones
      Excepting where 'tis gold.

'Think it over as you stand,
      For I tell you without fail,
If you haven't got into Fairyland
      You're not in Lewes Gaol.'

All night long they thought of it,
      And, come the dawn, they saw
They'd tumbled into a great old pit,
      At the bottom of Minepit Shaw.

And the keepers' hound had followed 'em close
      And broke her neck in the fall;
So they picked up their knives and their crossbows
      And buried the dog. That's all.

But whether the man was a poacher too
      Or a Pharisee so bold —
I reckon there's more things told than are true,
      And more things true than are told.

Rudyard Kipling

UNWELCOME

We were young, we were merry, we were very very wise,
      And the door stood open at our feast,
When there passed us a woman with the West in her eyes,
      And a man with his back to the East.

O, still grew the hearts that were beating so fast,
      The loudest voice was still.
The jest died away on our lips as they passed,
      And the rays of July struck chill.

The cups of red wine turned pale on the board,
 The white bread black as soot.
The hound forgot the hand of her lord,
 She fell down at his foot.

Low let me lie, where the dead dog lies,
 Ere I sit me down again at a feast,
When there passes a woman with the West in her eyes,
 And a man with his back to the East.

Mary Coleridge

THE LISTENERS

'Is there anybody there?' said the Traveller,
 Knocking on the moonlight door;
And his horse in the silence champed the grasses
 Of the forest's ferny floor:
And a bird flew up out of the turret,
 Above the Traveller's head:
And he smote upon the door again a second time;
 'Is there anybody there?' he said.
But no one descended to the Traveller;
 No head from the leaf-fringed sill
Leaned over and looked into his grey eyes,
 Where he stood perplexed and still.
But only a host of phantom listeners
 That dwelt in the lone house then
Stood listening in the quiet of the moonlight
 To that voice from the world of men:
Stood thronging the faint moonbeams on the dark stair,
 That goes down to the empty hall,
Harkening in an air stirred and shaken
 By the lonely Traveller's call.
And he felt in his heart their strangeness,
 Their stillness answering his cry,
While his horse moved, cropping the dark turf,
 'Neath the starred and leafy sky;

For he suddenly smote on the door, even
 Louder, and lifted his head:-
'Tell them I came, and no one answered,
 That I kept my word,' he said.
Never the least stir made the listeners,
 Though every word he spake
Fell echoing through the shadowiness of the still house
 From the one man left awake:
Ay, they heard his foot upon the stirrup,
 And the sound of iron on stone,
And how the silence surged softly backward,
 When the plunging hoofs were gone.

Walter de la Mare

TOM O' BEDLAM

The moon's my constant mistress,
 And the lovely owl my marrow;
  The flaming drake,
  And the night-crow, make
 Me music to my sorrow.

I know more than Apollo;
 For oft, when he lies sleeping,
  I behold the stars
  At mortal wars,
 And the rounded welkin weeping.

The moon embraces her shepherd,
 And the Queen of Love her warrior;
  While the first does horn
  The stars of the morn,
 And the next the heavenly farrier.

With a heart of furious fancies,
 Whereof I am commander:
  With a burning spear,
  And a horse of air,
 To the wilderness I wander;

With a Knight of ghosts and shadows,
. I summoned am to Tourney:
Ten leagues beyond
The wide world's end;
Methinks it is no journey.

LURIANA, LURILEE

Come out and climb the garden path
Luriana, Lurilee.
The China rose is all abloom
And buzzing with the yellow bee.
We'll swing you on the cedar bough,
Luriana, Lurilee.

I wonder if it seems to you,
Luriana, Lurilee,
That all the lives we ever lived
And all the lives to be,
Are full of trees and changing leaves,
Luriana, Lurilee.

How long it seems since you and I,
Luriana, Lurilee,
Roamed in the forest where our kind
Had just begun to be,
And laughed and chattered in the flowers,
Luriana, Lurilee.

How long since you and I went out,
Luriana, Lurilee,
To see the Kings go riding by
Over lawn and daisy lea,
With their palm leaves and cedar sheaves,
Luriana, Lurilee.

Swing, swing, on the cedar-bough,
   Luriana, Lurilee,
Till you sleep in a bramble heap
Or under a gloomy churchyard tree,
And then fly back to swing on a bough,
   Luriana, Lurilee.

Charles Elton

PUCK'S SONG

See you the ferny ride that steals
Into the oak-woods far?
O that was whence they hewed the keels
That rolled to Trafalgar.

And mark you where the ivy clings
To Bayham's mouldering walls?
O there we cast the stout railings
That stand around St. Paul's.

See you the dimpled track that runs
All hollow through the wheat?
O that was where they hauled the guns
That smote King Philip's fleet.

(Out of the Weald, the secret Weald,
Men sent in ancient years
The horse-shoes red at Flodden Field,
The arrows at Poitiers!)

See you our little mill that clacks,
So busy by the brook?
She has ground her corn and paid her tax
Ever since Domesday Book.

See you our stilly woods of oak,
And the dread ditch beside?
O that was where the Saxons broke
On the day that Harold died.

See you the windy levels spread
About the gates of Rye?
O that was where the Northmen fled,
When Alfred's ships came by.

See you our pastures wide and lone,
Where the red oxen browse?
O there was a City thronged and known,
Ere London boasted a house.

And see you, after rain, the trace
Of mound and ditch and wall?
O that was a Legion's camping-place,
When Caesar sailed from Gaul.

And see you marks that show and fade,
Like shadows on the Downs?
O they are the lines the Flint Men made,
To guard their wondrous towns.

Trackway and Camp and City lost,
Salt Marsh where now is corn —
Old Wars, old Peace, old Arts that cease,
And so was England born!

She is not any common Earth,
Water or wood or air,
But Merlin's Isle of Gramarye,
Where you and I will fare!

Rudyard Kipling

12

FACT AND FANCY,
TALK AND TALE

I tell this tale which is strictly true,
Just by way of convincing you . . .

KIPLING

THE BONNY EARL OF MURRAY

Ye Highlands and ye Lawlands,
   O where hae ye been?
They hae slain the Earl of Murray,
   And hae laid him on the green.

Now wae be to thee, Huntley!
   And whairfore did ye sae!
I bade you bring him wi' you,
   But forbade you him to slay.

He was a braw gallant,
   And he rid at the ring;
And the bonny Earl of Murray,
   O he might hae been a king!

He was a braw gallant,
   And he play'd at the ba';
And the bonny Earl of Murray
   Was the flower amang them a'!

He was a braw gallant,
   And he play'd at the gluve;
And the bonny Earl of Murray,
   O he was the Queen's luve!

O lang will his Lady
   Look owre the Castle Downe,
Ere she see the Earl of Murray
   Come sounding through the town!

Anon.

THE LAMENT OF BARBARA DOUGLAS

O waly, waly, up the bank,
    And waly, waly, doun the brae,
And waly, waly, yon burn-side,
    Where I and my Love wont to gae!

I lean'd my back unto an aik,
    I thocht it was a trustie tree;
But first it bow'd and syne it brak —
    Sae my true love did lichtlie me.

O waly, waly, gin love be bonnie
    A little time while it is new!
But when 'tis auld it waxeth cauld,
    And fades awa' like morning dew.

O wherefore should I busk my heid,
    Or wherefore should I kame my hair?
For my true Love has me forsook,
    And says he'll never lo'e me mair.

Now Arthur's Seat shall be my bed,
    The sheets shall ne'er be 'filed by me;
Saint Anton's well shall be my drink;
    Since my true Love has forsaken me.

Martinmas wind, when wilt thou blaw,
    And shake the green leaves aff the tree?
O gentle Death, when wilt thou come?
    For of my life I am wearie.

'Tis not the frost, that freezes fell,
    Nor blawing snaw's inclemencie,
'Tis not sic cauld that makes me cry;
    But my Love's heart grown cauld to me.

When we cam' in by Glasgow toun,
    We were a comely sicht to see;

My Love was clad in the black velvèt,
 And I mysel' in cramasie.

But had I wist, before I kist,
 That love had been sae ill to win,
I had lock'd my heart in a case o' gowd,
 And pinn'd it wi' a siller pin.

And O! if my young babe were born,
 And set upon the nurse's knee;
And I mysel' were dead and gane,
 And the green grass growing over me!

       Anon.

THE GYPSY COUNTESS

There cam' seven Egyptians on a day,
 And wow, but they sang bonny!
And they sang sae sweet, and sae very complete,
 Down cam' Earl Cassilis' lady.

She cam' tripping down the stair,
 And a' her maids before her;
As soon as they saw her weel-faur'd face
 They cast the glamourie owre her.

They gave to her the nutmeg,
 And they gave to her the ginger;
But she gave to them a far better thing,
 The seven gold rings off her fingers.

And when the Earl he did come home,
 Enquiring for his ladie,
One of the servants made this reply,
 'She's awa' with the gypsie laddie.'

255

'Come saddle for me the brown,' he said,
  'For the black was ne'er so speedy,
And I will travel night and day
  Till I find out my wanton ladie.'

'Will you come home, my dear?' he said,
  'O will you come home, my honey?
And by the point of my broad sword,
  A hand I'll ne'er lay on you.' . .

'Yestreen I rade this water deep,
  And my own gude lord beside me;
But this night I maun wet my little pretty feet
  With a wheen blackguards to wade me.

'Yestreen I lay on a good feather-bed,
  And my own wedded lord beyond me,
And to-night I'll lie in the ash-corner,
  With the gypsies all around me.

'They took off my high-heeled shoes,
  That were made of Spanish leather,
And I have put on coarse Lowland brogues,
  To trip it o'er the heather.

'The Earl of Cassilis is lying sick;
  Not one hair I'm sorry;
I'd rather have a kiss from Johnny Faa's lips
  Than all his gold and his money.'

Anon.

THE TWA CORBIES

  As I was walking all alane,
  I heard twa corbies making a mane:
  The tane unto the tither did say,
  'Whar sall we gang and dine the day?'

' — In behint yon auld fail dyke
I wot there lies a new-slain knight;
And naebody kens that he lies there
But his hawk, his hound, and his lady fair.

'His hound is to the hunting gane,
His hawk to fetch the wild-fowl hame,
His lady's ta'en anither mate,
So we may mak' our dinner sweet.

'Ye'll sit on his white hause-bane,
And I'll pike out his bonny blue e'en;
Wi' ae lock o' his gowden hair
We'll theek our nest when it grows bare.

'Mony a one for him maks mane,
But nane sall ken whar he is gane:
O'er his white banes, when they are bare,
The wind sall blaw for evermair.'

Anon.

BINNORIE

There were twa sisters sat in a bour;
  Binnorie, O binnorie!
There cam a knight to be their wooer,
  By the bonnie milldams o' Binnorie.

He courted the eldest with glove and ring,
But he lo'ed the youngest abune a' thing.

The eldest she was vexèd sair,
And sair envied her sister fair.

Upon a morning fair and clear,
She cried upon her sister dear:

'O sister, sister, tak my hand,
And we'll see our father's ships to land.'

She's ta'en her by the lily hand,
And led her down to the river-strand.

The youngest stood upon a stane,
The eldest cam and push'd her in.

'O sister, sister, reach your hand!
And ye sall be heir o' half my land:

'O sister, reach me but your glove!
And sweet William sall be your love.' —

'Foul fa' the hand that I should take;
It twin'd me o' my warldis make.

'Your cherry cheeks and your yellow hair
Gar'd me gang maiden evermair.'

Sometimes she sank, sometimes she swam,
Until she cam to the miller's dam.

Out then cam the miller's son,
And saw the fair maid soummin' in.

'O father, father, draw your dam!
There's either a mermaid or a milk-white swan.'

The miller hasted and drew his dam,
And there he found a drown'd woman.

You couldna see her middle sma',
Her gowden girdle was sae braw.

You couldna see her lily feet,
Her gowden fringes were sae deep.

You couldna see her yellow hair
For the strings o' pearls was twisted there.

You couldna see her fingers sma',
Wi' diamond rings they were cover'd a'.

And by there cam a harper fine,
That harpit to the king at dine.

And when he look'd that lady on,
He sigh'd and made a heavy moan.

He's made a harp of her breast-bane,
Whose sound wad melt a heart of stane.

He's ta'en three locks o' her yellow hair,
And wi' them strong his harp sae rare.

He went into her father's hall,
And there was the court assembled all.

He laid his harp upon a stane,
And straight it began to play by lane.

'O yonder sits my father, the King,
And yonder sits my mother, the Queen;

'And yonder stands my brother Hugh,
And by him my William, sweet and true.'

But the last tune that the harp play'd then —
   Binnorie, O binnorie!
Was, 'Woe to my sister, false Helèn!'
   By the bonnie milldams o' Binnorie.

                    Anon.

BONNY GEORGE CAMPBELL

Hie upon Hielands,
   And laigh upon Tay,
Bonny George Campbell
   Rade out on a day:
Saddled and bridled,
   Sae gallant to see,
Hame cam' his gude horse,
   But never cam' he.

Down ran his auld mither,
  Greetin' fu' sair;
Out ran his bonny bride,
  Reaving her hair;
'My meadow lies green,
  And my corn is unshorn,
My barn is to bigg,
  And my babe is unborn.'

Saddled and bridled
  And booted rade he;
A plume in his helmet,
  A sword at his knee;

But toom cam' his saddle
  A' bluidy to see,
O hame cam' his gude horse,
  But never cam' he!

Anon.

THE QUEEN'S MARIE

Marie Hamilton's to the kirk gane,
  Wi' ribbons in her hair;
The King thought mair o' Marie Hamilton
  Than ony that were there.

Marie Hamilton's to the kirk gane
  Wi' ribbons on her breast;
The King thought mair o' Marie Hamilton
  Than he listen'd to the priest.

Marie Hamilton's to the kirk gane,
  Wi' gloves upon her hands;
The King thought mair o' Marie Hamilton
  Than the Queen and a' her lands.

She hadna been about the King's court
   A month, but barely ane,
Till she was beloved by a' the King's court,
   And the King the only man.

She hadna been about the King's court
   A month, but barely three,
Till frae the King's court Marie Hamilton,
   Marie Hamilton durstna be.

The King is to the Abbey gane,
   To pu' the Abbey tree,
To scale the babe frae Marie's heart;
   But the thing it wadna be.

O she has row'd it in her apron,
   And set it on the sea —
'Gae sink ye or swim ye, bonny babe,
   Ye'se get nae mair o' me.'

Word is to the kitchen gane,
   And word is to the ha',
And word is to the noble room
   Amang the ladies a',
That Marie Hamilton's brought to bed,
   And the bonny babe's miss'd and awa'.

Scarcely had she lain down again,
   And scarcely fa'en asleep,
When up and started our gude Queen
   Just at her bed-feet;
Saying — 'Marie Hamilton, where's your babe?
   For I am sure I heard it greet.' —

'O no, O no, my noble Queen!
   Think no sic thing to be;
'Twas but a stitch into my side,
   And sair it troubles me!' —

'Get up, get up, Marie Hamilton:
    Get up and follow me;
For I am going to Edinburgh town,
    A rich wedding for to see.'

O slowly, slowly rase she up,
    And slowly put she on;
And slowly rade she out the way
    Wi' mony a weary groan.

The Queen was clad in scarlet,
    Her merry maids all in green;
And every town that they cam to,
    They took Marie for the Queen.

'Ride hooly, hooly, gentlemen,
    Ride hooly now wi' me!
For never, I am sure, a wearier burd
    Rade in your companie.'

But little wist Marie Hamilton,
    When she rade on the brown,
That she was gaen to Edinburgh town,
    And a' to be put down.

'Why weep ye sae, ye burgess wives,
    Why look ye sae on me?
O I am going to Edinburgh town,
    A rich wedding to see.

When she gaed up the tolbooth stairs,
    The corks frae her heels did flee;
And lang e'er she cam down again,
    She was condemned to die.

When she cam to the Netherbow port,
    She laugh'd loud laughters three;
But when she came to the gallows foot
    The tears blinded her e'e.

'Yestreen the Queen had four Maries,
    The night she'll hae but three;
Therè was Marie Seaton, and Marie Beaton,
    And Marie Carmichael, and me.

'O often have I dress'd my Queen,
    And put gowd upon her hair;
But now I've gotten for my reward
    The gallows to be my share.

'Often have I dress'd my Queen
    And often made her bed;
But now I've gotten for my reward
    The gallows tree to tread.

'I charge ye all, ye mariners,
    When ye sail owre the faem,
Let neither my father nor mother get wit
    But that I'm coming hame.

'I charge ye all, ye mariners,
    That sail upon the sea,
That neither my father nor mother get wit
    The dog's death I'm to die.

'For if my father and mother got wit,
    And my bold brethren three,
O mickle wad be the gude red blude
    This day wad be spilt for me!

'O little did my mother ken,
    The day she cradled me,
The lands I was to travel in
    Or the death I was to die!'

Anon.

HELEN OF KIRCONNELL

I wish I were where Helen lies,
Night and day on me she cries;
O that I were where Helen lies,
　　On fair Kirconnell lea!

Curst be the heart that thought the thought,
And curst the hand that fired the shot,
When in my arms burd Helen dropt,
　　And died to succour me!

O think na ye my heart was sair,
When my Love dropp'd and spak nae mair!
There did she swoon wi' meikle care,
　　On fair Kirconnell lea,

As I went down the water side,
None but my foe to be my guide,
None but my foe to be my guide,
　　On fair Kirconnell lea;

I lighted down my sword to draw,
I hackèd him in pieces sma',
I hackèd him in pieces sma',
　　For her sake that died for me.

O Helen fair, beyond compare!
I'll mak a garland o' thy hair,
Shall bind my heart for evermair,
　　Until the day I dee!

O that I were where Helen lies!
Night and day on me she cries;
Out of my bed she bids me rise,
　　Says, 'Haste, and come to me!'

O Helen fair! O Helen chaste!
If I were with thee, I'd be blest,
Where thou lies low and taks thy rest,
　　On fair Kirconnell lea.

I wish my grave were growing green,
A winding-sheet drawn owre my e'en,
And I in Helen's arms lying,
  On fair Kirconnell lea.

I wish I were where Helen lies!
Night and day on me she cries;
And I am weary of the skies,
  For her sake that died for me.

Anon.

THE FAREWELL

It was a' for our rightfu' King
  We left fair Scotland's strand;
It was a' for our rightfu' King
  We e'er saw Irish land,
    My dear —
  We e'er saw Irish land.

Now a' is done that men can do,
  And a' is done in vain;
My love and native land, farewell,
  For I maun cross the main,
    My dear —
  For I maun cross the main.

He turn'd him right and round about
  Upon the Irish shore;
And gae his bridle-reins a shake,
  With, Adieu for evermore,
    My dear —
  With, Adieu for evermore!

The sodger frae the wars returns,
  The sailor frae the main;
But I hae parted frae my love,

Never to meet again,
   My dear —
Never to meet again.

When day is gane, and night is come,
   And a' folk bound to sleep,
I think on him that's far awa',
   The lee-lang night, and weep,
      My dear —
   The lee-lang night, and weep.

Robert Burns

A LAMENT FOR FLODDEN

I've heard them lilting at our ewe-milking,
   Lasses a'lilting before dawn o' day;
But now they are moaning on ilka green loaning —
   The Flowers of the Forest are a' wede away.

At bughts, in the morning, nae blythe lads are scorning,
   Lasses are lonely and dowie and wae;
Nae daffing, nae gabbing, but sighing and sabbing,
   Ilk ane lifts her leglin and hies her away.

In hairst, at the shearing, nae youths now are jeering,
   Bandsters are lyart, and runkled, and gray:
At fair or at preaching, nae wooing, nae fleeching —
   The Flowers of the Forest are a' wede away.

At e'en, in the gloaming, nae swankies are roaming
   'Bout stacks wi' the lasses at bogle to play;
But ilk ane sits eerie, lamenting her dearie —
   The Flowers of the Forest are a' wede away.

Dool and wae for the order sent our lads to the Border!
   The English, for ance, by guile wan the day;
The Flowers of the Forest, that fought aye the foremost,
   The prime of our land, lie cauld in the clay.

We'll hear nae mair lilting at our ewe-milking;
  Women and bairns are heartless and wae;
Sighing and moaning on ilka green loaning —
  The Flowers of the Forest are a' wede away.

Jane Elliot

EDGEHILL FIGHT

Naked and grey the Cotswolds stand
  Beneath the autumn sun,
And the stubble-fields on either hand
  Where Stour and Avon run.
There is no change in the patient land
  That has bred us every one.

She should have passed in cloud and fire
  And saved us from this sin
Of war — red war — 'twixt child and sire,
  Household and kith and kin,
In the heart of a sleepy Midland shire,
  With the harvest scarcely in.

But there is no change as we meet at last
  On the brow-head or the plain,
And the raw astonished ranks stand fast
  To slay or to be slain
By the men they knew in the kindly past
  That shall never come again —

By the men they met at dance or chase,
  In the tavern or the hall,
At the justice-bench and the market-place,
  At the cudgel-play or brawl —
Of their own blood and speech and race,
  Comrades or neighbours all!

More bitter than death this day must prove
  Whichever way it go,
For the brothers of the maids we love
  Make ready to lay low
Their sisters' sweethearts, as we move
  Against our dearest foe.

Thank Heaven! At last the trumpets peal
  Before our strength gives way.
For King or for the Commonweal —
  No matter which they say,
The first dry rattle of new-drawn steel
  Changes the world to-day!

                    Rudyard Kipling

THE SORROWS OF WERTHER

Werther had a love for Charlotte
    Such as words could never utter;
Would you know how first he met her?
    She was cutting bread and butter.

Charlotte was a married lady,
    And a moral man was Werther,
And for all the wealth of Indies,
    Would do nothing for to hurt her.

So he sigh'd and pined and ogled,
    And his passion boil'd and bubbled,
Till he blew his silly brains out,
    And no more was by it troubled.

Charlotte, having seen his body
    Borne before her on a shutter,
Like a well-conducted person,
    Went on cutting bread and butter.

                                    W M Thackeray

THE WAR-SONG OF DINAS VAWR

The mountain sheep are sweeter,
But the valley sheep are fatter;
We therefore deemed it meeter
To carry off the latter.
We made an expedition;
We met a host, and quelled it;
We forced a strong position,
And killed the men who held it.

On Dyfed's richest calley,
Where herds of kine were brousing,
We made a mighty sally,
To furnish our carousing.
Fierce warriors rushed to meet us;
We met them, and o'erthrew them:
They struggled hard to beat us;
But we conquered them, and slew them.

As we drove our prize at leisure,
The king marched forth to catch us:
His rage surpassed all measure,
But his people could not match us.
He fled to his hall-pillars;
And, ere our force we led off,
Some sacked his house and cellars,
While others cut his head off.

We there, in strife bewild'ring,
Spilt blood enough to swim in:
We orphaned many children,
And widowed many women.
The eagles and the ravens
We glutted with our foemen;
The heroes and the cravens,
The spearmen and the bowmen.

We brought away from battle,
And much their land bemoaned them,
Two thousand head of cattle,
And the head of him who owned them:
Ednyfed, kind of Dyfed,
His head was borne before us;
His wine and beasts supplied our feasts,
And his overthrow, our chorus.

Thomas Love Peacock

GROWLTIGER'S LAST STAND

Growltiger was a Bravo Cat, who travelled on a barge:
In fact he was the roughest cat that ever roamed at large.
From Gravesend up to Oxford he pursued his evil aims,
Rejoicing in his title of 'The Terror of the Thames.'

His manners and appearance did not calculate to please;
His coat was torn and seedy, he was baggy at the knees;
One ear was somewhat missing, no need to tell you why,
And he scowled upon a hostile world from one forbidding
    eye.

The cottagers of Rotherhithe knew something of his fame;
At Hammersmith and Putney people shuddered at his name.
They would fortify the hen-house, lock up the silly goose,
When the rumour ran along the shore: GROWLTIGER'S ON
    THE LOOSE!

Woe to the weak canary, that fluttered from its cage;
Woe to the pampered Pekinese, that faced Growltiger's
    rage; .
Woe to the bristly Bandicoot, that lurks on foreign ships,
And woe to any Cat with whom Growltiger came to grips!

But most to Cats of foreign race his hatred had been vowed;
To Cats of foreign name and race no quarter was allowed.
The Persian and the Siamese regarded him with fear —
Because it was a Siamese had mauled his missing ear.

Now on a peaceful summer night, all nature seemed at play,
The tender moon was shining bright, the barge at Molesey
    lay.
All in the balmy moonlight it lay rocking on the tide —
And Growltiger was disposed to show his sentimental side.

His bucko mate, GRUMBUSKIN, long since had disappeared,
For to the Bell at Hampton he had gone to wet his beard;
And his bosun, TUMBLEBRUTUS, he too had stol'n away —
In the yard behind the Lion he was prowling for his prey.

In the forepeak of the vessel Growltiger sate alone,
Concentrating his attention on the Lady Griddlebone.
And his raffish crew were sleeping in their barrels and
    their bunks —
As the Siamese came creeping in their sampans and their
    junks.

Growltiger had no eye or ear for aught but Griddlebone,
And the Lady seemed enraptured by his manly baritone,
Disposed to relaxation, and awaiting no surprise —
But the moonlight shone reflected from a thousand bright
    blue eyes.

And closer still and closer the sampans circled round,
And yet from all the enemy there was not heard a sound.
The lovers sang their last duet, in danger of their lives —
For the foe was armed with toasting forks and cruel carving
    knives.

Then GILBERT gave the signal to his fierce Mongolian horde;
With a frightful burst of fireworks the Chinks they swarmed
    aboard.

Abandoning their sampans, and their pullaways and junks,
They battened down the hatches on the crew within their
    bunks.

Then Griddlebone she gave a screech, for she was badly
    skeered;
I am sorry to admit it, but she quickly disappeared.
She probably escaped with ease, I'm sure she was not
    drowned —
But a serried ring of flashing steel Growltiger did surround.

The ruthless foe pressed forward, in stubborn rank on rank;
Growltiger to his vast surprise was forced to walk the plank.
He who a hundred victims had driven to that drop,
At the end of all his crimes was forced to go ker-flip, ker-
    flop.

Oh there was joy in Wapping when the news flew through
    the land;
At Maidenhead and Henley there was dancing on the strand.
Rats were roasted whole at Brentford, and at Victoria Dock,
And a day of celebration was commanded in Bangkok.

T S Eliot

THE JOLLY YOUNG WATERMAN

And did you not hear of a jolly young Waterman,
    Who at Blackfriars Bridge us'd for to ply,
And he feather'd his oars with such skill and dexterity,
    Winning each heart and delighting each eye.
He looked so neat and row'd so steadily,
The maidens all flock'd to his boat so readily,
    And he eyed the young rogues with so charming an air,
    That this Waterman ne'er was in want of a fare.

What sights of fine folks he oft row'd in his wherry,
    'Twas cleaned out so nice and so painted withall,

273

He always was first when the fine city ladies,
    In a party to Ranelagh went, or Vauxhall.
And oft-times would they be giggling and leering,
But 'twas all one to Tom their jibing and jeering,
    For loving or liking he little did care,
    For this Waterman ne'er was in want of a fare.

And yet but to see how strangely things happen,
    As he row'd along thinking of nothing at all,
He was ply'd by a damsel so lovely and charming
    That she smil'd, and so straightway in love he did fall.
And would this young damsel e'en banish his sorrow,
He'd wed her to-night, before even to-morrow,
    And how should this Waterman ever know care,
    When he's married and never in want of a fare?

Charles Dibdin

I WAS A BUSTLE-MAKER ONCE, GIRLS

When I was a lad of twenty
    And was working in High Street, Ken.,
I made quite a pile in a very little while —
    I was a bustle-maker then.
Then there was work in plenty,
    And I was a thriving man;
But things have decayed in the bustle-making trade
    Since the bustle-making trade began.

I built bustles with a will then;
    I built bustles with a wit;
I built bustles as a Yankee hustles,
    Simply for the love of it.
I built bustles with a skill then
    Surpassed, they say, by none;
But those were the days when bustles were the craze,
    And now those days are done.

I was a bustle-maker once, girls,
    Many, many years ago;
I put my heart in the bustle-maker's art,
    And I don't mind saying so.
I may have had the brains of a dunce, girls;
    I may have had the mind of a muff;
I may have been plain and deficient in the brain,
    But I did know a bustle-maker's stuff.
I built bustles for the slender;
    I built bustles for the stout;
I built bustles for the girls with muscles
    And bustles for the girls without.
I built bustles by the thousands once
    In the good old days of yore;
But things have decayed in the bustle-making trade,
    And I don't build bustles any more.

Many were the models worn once;
    But mine were unique, 'tis said;
No rival design was so elegant as mine;
    I was a bustle-maker bred.
I was a bustle-maker born once —
    An artist through and through;
But things have decayed in the bustle-making trade,
    And what can a bustle-maker do?

I built bustles to enchant, girls;
    I built bustles to amaze;
I built bustles for the skirt that rustles,
    And bustles for the skirt that sways.
I built bustles for my aunt, girls,
    When other business fled;
But the bustle-maker can't make bustles for his aunt
    When a bustle-maker's aunt is dead.

I was a bustle-maker once, girls —
    Once in the days gone by,
I lost my heart to the bustle-maker's art,
    And that I don't deny.

I may have had the brains of a dunce, girls,
  As many men appear to suppose;
I may have been obtuse and of little other use,
  But I could build a bustle when I chose.
I built bustles for the bulging;
  I built bustles for the lithe;
I built bustles for the girls in Brussels
  And bustles for the girls in Hythe.
I built bustles for all Europe once,
  But I've been badly hit.
Things have decayed in the bustle-building trade,
  And that's the truth of it.

Patrick Barrington

THE 'MERGENCY MAN

He was lodging above in Coom,
And he'd the half of the bailiff's room.

'Till a black night came in Coomasaharn
A night of rains you'd swamp a star in.

'To-night,' says he, 'with the devil's weather
The hares itself will quit the heather.

'I'll catch my boys with a latch on the door,
And serve my process on near a score.'

The night was black at the fording place,
And the flood was up in a whitened race,
But devil a bit he'd turn his face.

Then the peelers said, 'Now mind your lepping,
How can you see the stones for stepping?

'We'll wash our hands of your bloody job.'
'Wash and welcome,' says he, 'begob.'

He made two leps with a run and dash,
Then the peelers heard a yell and splash;

And the 'mergency man in two days and a bit
Was found in the ebb tide stuck in a net.

J M Synge

OUR VILLAGE—BY A VILLAGER

Our village, that's to say not Miss Mitford's village, but our
   village of Bullock Smithy,
Is come into by an avenue of trees, three oak pollards, two
   elders and a withy;
And in the middle there's a green of about not exceeding an
   acre and a half;
It's common to all, and fed off by nineteen cows, six ponies,
   three horses, five asses, two foals, seven pigs and a calf.
Beside a pond in the middle, which is held by a similar sort
   of common law lease,
And contains twenty ducks, six drakes, three ganders, two
   dead dogs, four drowned kittens, and twelve geese.
Of course the green's cropt very close, and does famous for
   bowling when the village boys play at cricket;
Only some horse or pig, or cow, or great jackass, is sure to
   come and stand right before the wicket;
There's fifty-five private houses, let alone barns and
   workshops and pigstyes and poultry huts and such-like
      sheds;
With plenty of public-houses — two Foxes, one Green Man,
   three Bunch of Grapes, one Crown, and six King's Heads.
The Green Man is reckoned the best, as the only one that
   for love or money can raise
A postilion, a blue jacket, two deplorable lame white
   horses, and a ramshackled 'neat post-chaise.'

There's one parish church for all the people, whatsoever may
be their ranks in life or their degrees,
Except one very damp, small, dark, freezing-cold Methodist
Chapel of Ease;
And close by the churchyard there's a stone-mason's yard,
that when the time is seasonable
Will furnish with afflictions sore and marble urns and
cherubims very cheap and reasonable;
There's a cage, comfortable enough, I've been in it with old
Jack Jeffreys and Tom Pike;
For the Green Man next door will send you in ale, gin, or
anything else you like;
I can't speak of the stocks, as nothing remains of them but
the up-right post,
But the Pound is kept in repair for the sake of Cob's horse,
as is always there almost;
There's a smithy of course, where that queer sort of chap in
his way, old Joe Bradley,
Perpetually hammers and stammers, for he stutters and
shoes horses very badly.
There's a shop of sorts, that sells everything, kept by the
widow of Mr. Task.
But when you go there, it's ten to one she's out of everything
you ask;
You'll know her house by the swarm of boys, like flies,
about the old sugary cask;
There are six empty houses, and not so well papered inside
as out;
For the billstickers won't beware, but stick notices of sales
and election placards all about;
There's the Doctor's with a green door, where the garden pots
in the windows are seen,
A weakly monthly rose that won't blow, and a dead geranium,
and a tea-plant with five black leaves and one green.
As for hollyoaks at the cottage doors, and honey-suckle and
jasmines, you may go and whistle;
But the Tailor's front garden grows two cabbages, a dock, a
ha'porth of pennyroyal, two dandelions, and a thistle.

There are three small orchards — Mr. Busby's the school-
  master's is the chief —
With two pear-trees that don't bear; one plum and an apple,
  that every year is stripped by a thief.
There's another small day-school too, kept by the respectable
  Mrs. Gaby.
A select establishment, for six little boys and one big, and
  four little girls and a baby;
There's a rectory, with pointed gables and strange odd
  chimneys that never smokes,
For the rector don't live on his living like other Christian
  kind of folks;
There's a barber's once a week filled with rough, black-
  bearded, shock-headed churls,
And a window with two feminine men's heads, and two
  masculine ladies in false curls;
There's a butcher's, and a carpenter's, and a plumber's and a
  small greengrocer's and a baker,
But he won't bake on Sunday, and there's a sexton that's a
  coal-merchant besides, and an undertaker;
And a toyshop, but not a whole one, for a village can't
  compare with the London Shops;
One window sells drums, dolls, kites, carts, bats, Clout's balls,
  and the other sells malt and hops.
And Mrs. Brown, in domestic economy not to be a bit behind
  her betters,
Lets her house to a milliner, a watchmaker, a rat-catcher, a
  cobbler, lives in it herself, and it's the post-office for letters.
Now I've gone through all the village — aye, from end to end,
  save and except one more house,
But I haven't come to that — and I hope I never shall — and
  that's the Village Poor House!

Thomas Hood

THERE LIVED A KING

There lived a King, as I've been told,
In the wonder-working days of old,
When hearts were twice as good as gold,
   And twenty times as mellow.
Good-temper triumphed in his face,
And in his heart he found a place
For all the erring human race
   And every wretched fellow.
When he had Rhenish wine to drink
It made him very sad to think
That some, at junket or at jink,
   Must be content with toddy.
He wished all men as rich as he
(And he was rich as rich could be),
So to the top of every tree
   Promoted everybody.

Lord Chancellors were cheap as sprats,
And Bishops in their shovel hats
Were plentiful as tabby cats —
   In point of fact, too many.
Ambassadors cropped up like hay,
Prime Ministers and such as they
Grew like asparagus in May,
   And Dukes were three a penny.
On every side Field Marshals gleamed,
Small beer were Lords Lieutenant deemed,
With Admirals the ocean teemed
   All round his wide dominions.
And Party Leaders you might meet
In twos and threes in every street,
Maintaining, with no little heat,
   Their various opinions.

That King, although no one denies
His heart was of abnormal size,

Yet he'd have acted otherwise
    If he had been acuter.
The end is easily foretold,
When every blessed thing you hold
Is made of silver, or of gold,
    You long for simple pewter.
When you have nothing else to wear
But cloth of gold and satins rare,
For cloth of gold you cease to care —
    Up goes the price of shoddy.
In short, whoever you may be,
To this conclusion you'll agree,
When everyone is someboddee,
    Then no one's anybody.

                                    W S Gilbert

MY LAST DUCHESS

That's my last Duchess painted on the wall,
Looking as if she were alive; I call
That piece a wonder, now: Frà Pandolf's hands
Worked busily a day, and there she stands.
Will't please you sit and look at her? I said
'Frà Pandolf' by design, for never read
Strangers like you that pictured countenance,
The depth and passion of its earnest glance,
But to myself they turned (since none puts by
The curtain I have drawn for you, but I)
And seemed as they would ask me, if they durst,
How such a glance came there; so, not the first
Are you to turn and ask thus. Sir, 't was not
Her husband's presence only, called that spot
Of joy into the Duchess' cheek: perhaps
Frà Pandolf chanced to say 'Her mantle laps
Over my Lady's wrist too much,' or 'Paint
Must never hope to reproduce the faint
Half-flush that dies along her throat;' such stuff

Was courtesy, she thought, and cause enough
For calling up that spot of joy. She had
A heart ... how shall I say? ... too soon made glad,
Too easily impressed; she liked whate'er
She looked on, and her looks went everywhere.
Sir, 't was all one! My favour at her breast,
The dropping of the daylight in the West,
The bough of cherries some officious fool
Broke in the orchard for her, the white mule
She rode with round the terrace — all and each
Would draw from her alike the approving speech,
Or blush, at least. She thanked men, — good; but thanked
Somehow ... I know not how ... as if she ranked
My gift of a nine-hundred-years-old name
With anybody's gift. Who'd stop to blame
This sort of trifling? Even had you skill
In speech — (which I have not) — to make your will
Quite clear to such an one, and say 'Just this
Or that in you disgusts me; here you miss,
Or there exceed the mark' — and if she let
Herself be lessoned so, nor plainly set
Her wits to yours, forsooth, and made excuse,
— E'en then would be some stooping, and I chuse
Never to stoop. Oh, Sir, she smiled, no doubt,
Whene'er I passed her; but who passed without
Much the same smile? This grew; I gave commands;
Then all smiles stopped together. There she stands
As if alive. Will't please you rise? We'll meet
The company below, then. I repeat,
The Count your Master's known munificence
Is ample warrant that no just pretence
Of mine for dowry will be disallowed;
Though his fair daughter's self, as I avowed
At starting, is my object. Nay, we'll go
Together down, Sir! Notice Neptune, though,
Taming a sea-horse, thought a rarity,
Which Claus of Innsbruck cast in bronze for me.

Robert Browning

13

BEHOLD MORTALITY

In this little Urn is laid
Prewdence Baldwin (once my maid)
From whose happy spark here let
Spring the purple Violet

HERRICK

ON A QUIET CONSCIENCE

Close thine eyes, and sleep secure;
Thy soul is safe, thy body sure.
He that guards thee, he that keeps,
Never slumbers, never sleeps.
A quiet conscience in the breast
Has only peace, has only rest.
The wisest and the mirth of kings
Are out of tune unless she sings:
Then close thine eyes in peace and sleep secure,
No sleep so sweet as thine, no rest so sure.

King Charles I

A FAREWELL TO ARMS
To Queen Elizabeth

His golden locks Time hath to silver turn'd;
  O Time too swift, O swiftness never ceasing!
His youth 'gainst time and age hath ever spurn'd,
  But spurn'd in vain; youth waneth by increasing:
Beauty, strength, youth, are flowers but fading seen;
Duty, faith, love, are roots, and ever green.

His helmet now shall make a hive for bees;
  And, lovers' sonnets turn'd to holy psalms,
A man-at-arms must now serve on his knees,
  And feed on prayers, which are Age his alms:
But though from court to cottage he depart,
His Saint is sure of his unspotted heart.

And when he saddest sits in homely cell,
  He'll teach his swains this carol for a song, —
'Blest be the hearts that wish my sovereign well,
  Curst be the souls that think her any wrong.'
Goddess, allow this aged man his right
To be your beadsman now that was your knight.

George Peele

TO DIANEME

Sweet, be not proud of those two eyes
Which starlike sparkle in their skies;
Nor be you proud that you can see
All hearts your captives, yours yet free;
Be you not proud of that rich hair
Which wantons with the love-sick air;
Whenas that ruby which you wear,
Sunk from the tip of your soft ear,
Will last to be a precious stone
When all your world of beauty's gone.

Robert Herrick

DIRGE FROM 'CYMBELINE'

Fear no more the heat o' the sun,
    Nor the furious winter's rages;
Thou thy worldly task hast done,
    Home art gone, and ta'en thy wages:
Golden lads and girls all must,
As chimney-sweepers, come to dust.

Fear no more the frown o' the great,
    Thou art past the tyrant's stroke;
Care no more to clothe and eat;
    To thee the reed is as the oak:
The sceptre, learning, physic, must
All follow this, and come to dust.

Fear no more the lightning-flash,
    Nor the all-dreaded thunder-stone;
Fear not slander, censure rash;
    Thou hast finish'd joy and moan:
All lovers young, all lovers must
Consign to thee, and come to dust.

No exorciser harm thee!
Nor no witchcraft charm thee!
Ghost unlaid forbear thee!
Nothing ill come near thee!
Quiet consummation have;
And renownèd be thy grave!

William Shakespeare

'WEEP YOU NO MORE'

Weep you no more, sad fountains;
   What need you flow so fast?
Look how the snowy mountains
   Heaven's sun doth gently waste!
But my Sun's heavenly eyes
    View not your weeping,
   That now lies sleeping
Softly, now softly lies
   Sleeping.

Sleep is a reconciling,
   A rest that peace begets;
Doth not the sun rise smiling
   When fair at even he sets?
Rest you then, rest, sad eyes!
    Melt not in weeping,
   While she lies sleeping
Softly, now softly lies
   Sleeping.

Anon.

LIFE

I made a posie while the day ran by:
Here will I smell my remnant out, and tie
  My life within this band;
But Time did becken to the flow'rs, and they
By noon most cunningly did steal away,
  And wither'd in my hand.

My hand was next to them, and then my heart;
I took, without more thinking, in good part
  Time's gentle admonition;
Who did so sweetly Death's sad taste convey,
Making my minde to smell my fatall day,
  Yet sugring the suspicion.

Farewell, deare flow'rs; sweetly your time ye spent,
Fit while ye lived for smell or ornament,
  And after death for cures.
I follow straight, without complaints or grief;
Since if my scent be good, I care not if
  It be as short as yours.

George Herbert

'THE GLORIES OF OUR BLOOD AND STATE

The glories of our blood and state
  Are shadows, not substantial things;
There is no armour against Fate;
  Death lays his icy hand on kings.
    Sceptre and Crown
    Must tumble down,
  And in the dust be equal made
With the poor crookéd scythe and spade.

Some men with swords may reap the field,
  And plant fresh laurels where they kill:
But their strong nerves at last must yield;
  They tame but one another still:
    Early or late
    They stoop to fate,
  And must give up their murmuring breath
  When they, pale captives, creep to death.

The garlands wither on your brow;
  Then boast no more your mighty deeds!
Upon Death's purple altar now
  See where the victor-victim bleeds.
    Your heads must come
    To the cold tomb:
  Only the actions of the just
  Smell sweet and blossom in their dust.

James Shirley

VERSES FOUND IN HIS BIBLE

Even such is Time, that takes in trust
  Our youth, our joys, our all we have,
And pays us but with earth and dust;
  Who in the dark and silent grave,
When we have wander'd all our ways,
Shuts up the story of our days;
But from this earth, this grave, this dust,
My God shall raise me up, I trust.

Sir Walter Raleigh

From 'KING RICHARD II'

Aumerle.   Where is the duke my father with his power?
K. Richard. No matter where, of comfort no man speak:
Let's talk of graves, of worms, and epitaphs,
Make dust our paper, and with rainy eyes
Write sorrow on the bosom of the earth ...

Let's choose executors and talk of wills:
And yet not so, for what can we bequeath,
Save our deposed bodies to the ground?
Our lands, our lives, and all are Bolingbroke's,
And nothing can we call our own, but death;
And that small model of the barren earth,
Which serves as paste and cover to our bones.
For God's sake let us sit upon the ground,
And tell sad stories of the death of kings –
How some have been deposed, some slain in war,
Some haunted by the ghosts they have deposed,
Some poisoned by their wives, some sleeping killed;
All murdered – for within the hollow crown
That rounds the mortal temples of a king,
Keeps Death his court, and there the antic sits,
Scoffing his state and grinning at his pomp,
Allowing him a breath, a little scene,
To monarchize, be feared, and kill with looks,
Infusing him with self and vain conceit,
As if this flesh which walls about our life,
Were brass impregnable: and humoured thus,
Comes at the last, and with a little pin
Bores through his castle wall, and farewell king!

William Shakespeare

ASPATIA'S SONG

Lay a garland on my herse
    Of the dismal yew;
Maidens, willow branches bear;
    Say, I died true.

My love was false, but I was firm
    From my hour of birth.
Upon my buried body lie
    Lightly, gentle earth!

John Fletcher

From ANTONY AND CLEOPATRA

Antony: The miserable change now at my end
Lament nor sorrow at; but please your thoughts
In feeding them with those my former fortunes
Wherein I lived ... the greatest prince o'th'world,
The noblest ... and do now not basely die,
Not cowardly put off my helmet to
My countryman ... a Roman by a Roman
Valiantly vanquished. Now my spirit is going,
I can no more.
Cleopatra: Noblest of men, wood'st die?
Hast thou no care of me? shall I abide
In this dull world, which in thy absence is
No better than a sty? O, see, my women ...
                Antony dies
The crown o'th'earth doth melt. My lord!
O, withered is the garland of the war,
The soldier's pole is fall'n: young boys and girls
Are level now with men: the odds is gone,
And there is nothing left remarkable
Beneath the visiting moon.

William Shakespeare

Mortality, behold and fear!
What a change of flesh is here!
Think how many royal bones
Sleep within this heap of stones:
Here they lie had realms and lands,
Who now want strength to stir their hands:
Where from their pulpits seal'd with dust
They preach, 'In greatness is no trust.'
Here's an acre sown indeed
With the richest, royall'st seed
That the earth did e'er suck in
Since the first man died for sin:
Here the bones of birth have cried —
'Though gods they were, as men they died.'
Here are sands, ignoble things,
Dropt from the ruin'd sides of kings;
Here's a world of pomp and state,
Buried in dust, once dead by fate.

Francis Beaumont

FROM 'DAPHNAIDA'

She fell away in her first ages spring,
Whil'st yet her leafe was greene, and fresh her rinde,
And whil'st her braunch faire blossomes foorth did bring,
She fell away against all course of kinde.
For age to dye is right, but youth is wrong;
She fell away like fruit blowne downe with winde.
Weepe, Shepheard! weepe, to make my undersong . . . .

Yet fell she not as one enforst to dye,
Ne dyde with dread and grudging discontent,
But as one toyld with travaile downe doth lye,

So lay she downe, as if to sleepe she went,
And closed her eyes with carelesse quietnesse;
The whiles soft death away her spirit hent,
And soule assoyld from sinfull fleshlinesse . . . .

How happie was I when I saw her leade
The Shepheards daughters dauncing in a rownd!
How trimly would she trace and softly tread
The tender grasse, with rosie garland crownd!
And when she list advance her heavenly voyce,
Both Nymphes and Muses nigh she made astownd,
And flocks and shepheards caus̀ed to rejoyce.

But now, ye Shepheard lasses! who shall lead
Your wandring troupes, or sing your virelayes?
Or who shall dight your bowres, sith she is dead
That was the Lady of your holy-dayes?
Let now your blisse be turnèd into bale,
And into plaints convert your joyous playes,
And with the same fill every hill and dale.

Edmund Spenser

From 'THE FAERIE QUEENE'

What if some little pain the passage have,
That makes frail flesh to fear the bitter wave?
Is not short pain well borne, that brings long ease,
And lays the soul to sleep in quiet grave?
Sleep after toil, port after stormy seas,
Ease after war, death after life does greatly please.

Edmund Spenser

THE UNQUIET GRAVE

'The wind doth blow to-day, my love,
   And a few small drops of rain;
I never had but one true-love;
   In cold grave she was lain.

'I'll do as much for my true-love
   As any young man may;
I'll sit and mourn all at her grave
   For a twelvemonth and a day.'

The twelvemonth and a day being up,
   The dead began to speak:
'Oh who sits weeping on my grave,
   And will not let me sleep?' —

''Tis I, my love, sits on your grave,
   And will not let you sleep;
For I crave one kiss of your clay-cold lips
   And that is all I seek.' —

'You crave one kiss of my clay-cold lips;
   But my breath smells earthy strong;
If you have one kiss of my clay-cold lips,
   Your time will not be long.

''Tis down in yonder garden green,
   Love, where we used to walk,
The finest flower that ere was seen
   Is wither'd to a stalk.

'The stalk is wither'd dry, my love,
   So will our hearts decay;
So make yourself content, my love,
   Till God calls you away.'

Anon.

REMEMBER

Remember me when I am gone away,
   Gone far away into the silent land;
   When you can no more hold me by the hand,
Nor I half turn to go, yet turning stay.
Remember me when no more day by day
   You tell me of our future that you plann'd:
   Only remember me; you understand
It will be late to counsel then or pray.
Yet if you should forget me for a while
   And afterwards remember, do not grieve:
   For if the darkness and corruption leave
   A vestige of the thoughts that once I had,
Better by far you should forget and smile
   Than that you should remember and be sad.

Christina Rossetti

THE FUNERAL

Whoever comes to shroud me, do not harm
   Nor question much
That subtle wreath of hair, which crowns my arm;
The mystery, the sign you must not touch,
   For 'tis my outward Soul,
Viceroy to that, which then to heaven being gone,
   Will leave this to control,
And keep these limbs, her Provinces, from dissolution.

For if the sinewy thread my brain lets fall
   Through every part,
Can tie those parts, and make me one of all;
These hairs which upward grew, and strength and art
   Have from a better brain,

Can better do't; except she meant that I
    By this should know my pain,
As prisoners then are manacled, when they're condemn'd to
    die.

Whate'er she meant by it, bury it with me,
    For since I am
Love's martyr, it might breed idolatry,
If into others' hands these Reliques came;
    As 'twas humility
To afford to it all that a Soul can do,
    So, 'tis some bravery,
That since you would save none of me, I bury some of you.

                                        John Donne

THE RELIQUE

    When my grave is broke up again
    Some second guest to entertain,
    (For graves have learn'd that woman-head
    To be to more than one a Bed)
        And he that digs it, spies
A bracelet of bright hair about the bone,
        Will he not let us alone,
And think that there a loving couple lies,
Who thought that this device might be some way
To make their souls, at the last busy day,
Meet at this grave, and make a little stay?

    If this fall in a time, or land,
    Where mis-devotion doth command,
    Then, he that digs us up, will bring
    Us, to the Bishop and the King
        To make us Reliques; then
Thou shalt be a Mary Magdalen, and I
        A something else thereby;

All women shall adore us, and some men;
And since at such time, miracles are sought,
I would have that age by this paper taught
What miracles we harmless lovers wrought.

First, we lov'd well and faithfully,
Yet knew not what we lov'd, nor why,
Difference of sex no more we knew,
Than our Guardian Angels do;
Coming and going, we
Perchance might kiss, but not between those meals;
Our hands ne'er touched the seals,
Which nature, injur'd by late law, sets free:
These miracles we did; but now alas,
All measure, and all language, I should pass,
Should I tell what a miracle she was.

John Donne

AT THE GRAVE OF HENRY VAUGHAN

Above the voiceful windings of a river
An old green slab of simply graven stone
Shuns notice, overshadowed by a yew.
Here Vaughan lies dead, whose name flows on for ever
Through pastures of the spirit washed with dew
And starlit with eternities unknown.

Here sleeps the Silurist; the loved physician;
The face that left no portraiture behind;
The skull that housed white angels and had vision
Of daybreak through the gateways of the mind.
Here faith and mercy, wisdom and humility
(Whose influence shall prevail for evermore)
Shine. And this lowly grave tells Heaven's tranquillity.
And here stand I, a suppliant at the door.

Siegfried Sassoon

TITHONUS

The woods decay, the woods decay and fall,
The vapours weep their burthen to the ground,
Man comes and tills the field and lies beneath,
And after many a summer dies the swan.
Me only cruel immortality
Consumes: I wither slowly in thine arms,
Here at the quiet limit of the world,
A white-hair'd shadow roaming like a dream
The ever-silent spaces of the East,
Far-folded mists, and gleaming halls of morn.

Alas! for this gray shadow, once a man —
So glorious in his beauty and thy choice,
Who madest him thy chosen, that he seem'd
To his great heart none other than a God!
I ask'd thee, 'Give me immortality.'
Then didst thou grant mine asking with a smile,
Like wealthy men who care not how they give.
But thy strong Hours indignant work'd their wills,
And beat me down and marr'd and wasted me,
And tho' they could not end me, left me maim'd
To dwell in presence of immortal youth,
Immortal age beside immortal youth,
And all I was, in ashes. Can thy love,
Thy beauty, make amends, tho' even now,
Close over us, the silver star, thy guide,
Shines in those tremulous eyes that fill with tears
To hear me? Let me go: take back thy gift:
Why should a man desire in any way
To vary from the kindly race of men,
Or pass beyond the goal of ordinance
Where all should pause, as is most meet for all?

A soft air fans the cloud apart; there comes
A glimpse of that dark world where I was born.
Once more the old mysterious glimmer steals
From thy pure brows, and from thy shoulders pure,

And bosom beating with a heart renew'd.
Thy sheek begins to redden thro' the gloom,
Thy sweet eyes brighten slowly close to mine,
Ere yet they blind the stars, and the wild team
Which love thee, yearning for thy yoke, arise,
And shake the darkness from their loosen'd manes,
And beat the twilight into flakes of fire.

Lo! ever thus thou growest beautiful
In silence, then before thine answer given
Departest, and thy tears are on my cheek.

Why wilt thou ever scare me with thy tears,
And make me tremble lest a saying learnt,
In days far-off, on that dark earth, be true?
'The Gods themselves cannot recall their gifts.'

Ay me! ay me! with what another heart
In days far-off, and with what other eyes
I used to watch — if I be he that watch'd —
The lucid outline forming round thee; saw
The dim curls kindle into sunny rings;
Changed with thy mystic change, and felt my blood
Glow with the glow that slowly crimson'd all
Thy presence and thy portals, while I lay,
Mouth, forehead, eyelids, growing dewy-warm
With kisses balmier than half-opening buds
Of April, and could hear the lips that kiss'd
Whispering I knew not what of wild and sweet,
Like that strange song I heard Apollo sing,
While Ilion like a mist rose into towers.

Yet hold me not for ever in thine East:
How can my nature longer mix with thine?
Coldly thy rosy shadows bathe me, cold
Are all thy lights, and cold my wrinkled feet
Upon thy glimmering thresholds, when the steam
Floats up from those dim fields about the homes
Of happy men that have the power to die,

And grassy barrows of the happier dead.
Release me, and restore me to the ground;
Thou seest all things, thou wilt see my grave:
Thou wilt renew thy beauty morn by morn;
I earth in earth forget these empty courts,
And thee returning on thy silver wheels.

Alfred Tennyson

'A SLUMBER DID MY SPIRIT SEAL'

A slumber did my spirit seal;
   I had no human fears:
She seemed a thing that could not feel
   The touch of earthly years.

No motion has she now, no force;
   She neither hears nor sees;
Rolled round in earth's diurnal course,
   With rocks, and stones, and trees.

William Wordsworth

DURING WIND AND RAIN

   They sing their dearest songs —
   He, she, all of them — yea,
   Treble and tenor and bass,
     And one to play;
   With the candles mooning each face ....
     Ah, no; the years O!
How the sick leaves reel down in throngs!

They clear the creeping moss —
Elders and juniors — aye,
Making the pathways neat
 And the garden gay;
And they build a shady seat . . . .
 Ah, no; the years, the years;
See, the white storm-birds wing across!

They are blithely breakfasting all —
Men and maidens — yea,
Under the summer tree,
 With a glimpse of the bay,
While pet fowl come to the knee . . . .
 Ah, no; the years O!
And the rotten rose is ript from the wall.

They change to a high new house,
He, she, all of them — aye,
Clocks and carpets and chairs
 On the lawn all day,
And brightest things that are their . . . .
 Ah, no; the years, the years;
Down their carved names the rain-drop ploughs.

Thomas Hardy

REGRET NOT ME

Regret not me;
Beneath the sunny tree
I lie uncaring, slumbering peacefully.

Swift as the light
I flew my faery flight;
Ecstatically I move, and feared no night.

I did not know
That heydays fade and go,
But deemed that what was would be always so.

I skipped at morn
Between the yellowing corn,
Thinking it good and glorious to be born.

I ran at eves
Among the piled-up sheaves,
Dreaming, 'I grieve not, therefore nothing grieves.'

Now soon will come
The apple, pear, and plum,
And hinds will sing, and autumn insects hum.

Again you will fare
To cider-makings rare,
And junketings; but I shall not be there.

Yet gaily sing
Until the pewter ring
Those songs we sang when we went gipsying.

And lightly dance
Some triple-timed romance
In coupled figures, and forget mischance;

And mourn not me
Beneath the yellowing tree;
For I shall mind not, slumbering peacefully.

Thomas Hardy

He drowsed and was aware of silence heaped
Round him, unshaken as the steadfast walls;
Aqueous like floating rays of amber light,
Soaring and quivering in the wings of sleep.
Silence and safety; and his mortal shore
Lipped by the inward, moonless waves of death.

Some one was holding water to his mouth.
He swallowed, unresisting; moaned and dropped
Through crimson gloom to darkness; and forgot
The opiate throb and ache that was his wound.
Water — calm, sliding green above the weir;
Water — a sky-lit alley for his boat,
Bird-voiced, and bordered with reflected flowers
And shaken hues of summer: drifting down,
He dipped contented oars, and sighed, and slept.

Night, with a gust of wind, was in the ward,
Blowing the curtain to a glimmering curve.
Night. He was blind; he could not see the stars
Glinting among the wraiths of wandering cloud;
Queer blots of colour, purple, scarlet, green,
Flickered and faded in his drowning eyes.

Rain; he could hear it rustling through the dark;
Fragrance and passionless music woven as one;
Warm rain on drooping roses; pattering showers
That soak the woods; not the harsh rain that sweeps
Behind the thunder, but a trickling peace
Gently and slowly washing life away.

                    *   *   *

He stirred, shifting his body; then the pain
Leaped like a prowling beast, and gripped and tore
His groping dreams with grinding claws and fangs.
But someone was beside him; soon he lay
Shuddering because that evil thing had passed.

And Death, who'd stepped toward him, paused and stared.

Light many lamps and gather round his bed.
Lend him your eyes, warm blood, and will to live.
Speak to him; rouse him; you may save him yet.
He's young, he hated war; how should he die
When cruel old campaigners win safe through?

But Death replied: 'I choose him.' So he went.
And there was silence in the summer night;
Silence and safety; and the veils of sleep.
Then, far away, the thudding of the guns.

Siegfried Sassoon

OZYMANDIAS

I met a traveller from an antique land
Who said: Two vast and trunkless legs of stone
Stand in the desert. Near them, on the sand,
Half sunk, a shattered visage lies, whose frown,
And wrinkled lip, and sneer of cold command,
Tell that its sculptor well those passions read
Which yet survive, stamped on these lifeless things,
The hand that mocked them, and the heart that fed:
And on the pedestal these words appear:
'My name is Ozymandias, king of kings:
Look on my works, ye Mighty, and despair!'
Nothing beside remains. Round the decay
Of that colossal wreck, boundless and bare
The lone and level sands stretch far away.

Percy Bysshe Shelley

TO HIS DYING BROTHER,
MASTER WILLIAM HERRICK

Life of my life, take not so soon thy flight,
But stay the time till we have bade good-night.
Thou hast both wind and tide with thee; thy way
As soon despatch'd is by the night as day.
Let us not then so rudely henceforth go
Till we have wept, kissed, sigh'd, shook hands or so.
There's pain in parting, and a kind of hell,
When once true lovers take their last farewell.
What! shall we two our endless leaves take here
Without a sad look or a solemn tear?
He knows not love that hath not this truth proved.
Love is most loth to leave the thing beloved.
Pay we our vows and go; yet when we part,
Then, even then, I will bequeath my heart
Into thy loving hands; for I'll keep none
To warm my breast when thou, my pulse, art gone.
No, here I'll last, and walk (a harmless shade)
About this urn wherein thy dust is laid,
To guard it so as nothing here shall be
Heavy to hurt those sacred seeds of thee.

Robert Herrick

From His 'EXEQUY ON HIS WIFE'

    Sleep on, my Love, in thy cold bed
Never to be disquieted!
My last goodnight! Thou wilt not wake
Till I thy fate shall overtake:
Till age, or grief, or sickness must
Marry my body to that dust
It so much loves; and fill the room
My heart keeps empty in thy tomb.

Stay for me there: I will not fail
To meet thee in that hollow vale.
And think not much of my delay:
I am already on the way,
And follow thee with all the speed
Desire can make, or sorrows breed.
Each minute is a short degree
And every hour a step towards thee . . . .
　　'Tis true — with shame and grief I yield —
Thou, like the van, first took'st the field;
And gotten hast the victory
In thus adventuring to die
Before me, whose more years might crave
A just precedence in the grave.
But hark! my pulse, like a soft drum,
Beats my approach, tells thee I come;
And slow howe'er my marches be
I shall at last sit down by thee.

Henry King

DIRGE FROM 'TWELFTH NIGHT'

Come away, come away, death,
　And in sad cypres let me be laid;
Fly away, fly away, breath;
　I am slain by a fair cruel maid.
My shroud of white, stuck all with yew,
　　O prepare it!
My part of death, no one so true
　　Did share it.

Not a flower, not a flower sweet,
　On my black coffin let there be strown;
Not a friend, not a friend greet
　My poor corse, where my bones shall be thrown:

A thousand thousand sighs to save,
        Lay me, O, where
Sad true lover never find my grave
        To weep there!'

                        William Shakespeare

TO AN OLD LADY DEAD

Old lady, when last year I sipped your tea
And wooed you with my deference to discuss
The elegance of your embroidery,
I felt no forethought of our meeting thus.
Last week your age was 'almost eighty-three.'
To-day you own the eternal over-plus.
These moments are 'experience' for me;
But not for you; not for a mutual 'us.'

I visit you unwelcomed; you've no time
Left to employ in afternoon politeness.
You've only Heaven's great stairway now to climb,
And your long load of years has changed to lightness.
When Oxford belfries chime you do not hear,
Nor in this mellow-toned autumnal brightness
Observe an English-School-like atmosphere . . . .
You have inherited everlasting whiteness.

You lived your life in grove and garden shady
Of social Academe, good talk and taste:
But now you are a very quiet old lady,
Stiff, sacrosanct, and alabaster-faced.
And, while I tip-toe awe-struck from your room,
I fail to synthesize your earth-success
With this, your semblance to a sculptured tomb
That clasps a rosary of nothingness.

                        Siegfried Sassoon

306

In the hour of my distress,
When temptations me oppress,
And when I my sins confess,
  Sweet Spirit comfort me!

When I lie within my bed,
Sick in heart, and sick in head,
And with doubts discomforted,
  Sweet Spirit comfort me!

When the house doth sigh and weep,
And the world is drown'd in sleep,
Yet mine eyes the watch do keep;
  Sweet Spirit comfort me!

When the artless Doctor sees
No one hope, but of his fees,
And his skill runs on the lees;
  Sweet Spirit comfort me!

When his potion and his pill,
His, or none, or little skill,
Meet for nothing, but to kill;
   Sweet Spirit comfort me!

     *   *   *

When the passing-bell doth toll,
And the Furies in a shoal
Come to fright a parting soul;
   Sweet Spirit comfort me!

When the tapers now burn blue,
And the comforters are few,
And that number more than true;
   Sweet Spirit comfort me!

When the Priest his last hath pray'd,
And I nod to what is said,
'Cause my speech is now decay'd;
   Sweet Spirit comfort me!

When, (God knows) I'm toss'd about,
Either with despair or doubt;
Yet before the glass be out,
   Sweet Spirit comfort me!

When the Tempter me pursu'th
With the sins of all my youth,
And half damns me with untruth;
   Sweet Spirit comfort me!

When the flames and hellish cries
Fright mine ears and fright mine eyes,
And all terrors me surprise;
   Sweet Spirit comfort me!

When the Judgment is reveal'd,
And that open'd which was seal'd,
When to Thee I have appeal'd;
   Sweet Spirit comfort me!

Robert Herrick

14
EPIGRAMS, EPIGRAPHS
& EPITAPHS

Swans sing before they die – 'twere no bad thing
Should certain persons die before they sing

COLERIDGE

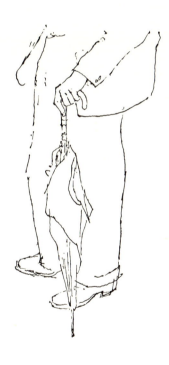

EPIGRAM

ENGRAVED ON THE COLLAR OF A DOG
WHICH I GAVE TO HIS ROYAL HIGHNESS

I am his Highness' dog at Kew;
Pray tell me, sir, whose dog are you?

Alexander Pope

*

PASSIONS

Passions are liken'd best to floods and streams:
  The shallow murmur, but the deep are dumb;
So, when affection yields discourse, it seems
  The bottom is but shallow whence they come.
They that are rich in words, in words discover
That they are poor in that which makes a lover.

Sir Walter Raleigh

*

ADAM AND EVE

Whilst Adam slept, Eve from his side arose:
Strange his first sleep should be his last repose.

Anon.

*

EPIGRAM

My soul, sit thou a patient looker-on;
Judge not the play before the play is done:
Her plot hath many changes; every day
Speaks a new scene; the last act crowns the play.

Francis Quarles

DIRCE

Stand close around, ye Stygian set,
    With Dirce in one boat convey'd!
Or Charon, seeing, may forget
    That he is old and she a shade.

Walter Savage Landor

*

YOU BEAT YOUR PATE

You beat your pate, and fancy wit will come:
Knock as you please, there's nobody at home.

Alexander Pope

*

THE TURNIP CRIER

If the man who turnips cries,
Cry not when his father dies,
'Tis a proof that he had rather
Have a turnip than his father.

Samuel Johnson

*

'HOW DAUR YE CALL ME OWLET FACE'

How daur ye call me owlet face
Ye ugly glowering spectre?
My face is but the keeking glass
And there ye saw your picter.

Robert Burns

*

ON CROMEK

A petty sneaking knave I knew —
O! Mr. Cromek, how do ye do?

William Blake

311

JUST AND UNJUST

The rain it raineth on the just
  And also on the unjust fella;
But chiefly on the just, because
  The unjust steals the just's umbrella.

Lord Bowen

*

DAVID AND SOLOMON

King David and King Solomon
  Led merry, merry lives,
With many, many lady friends
  And many, many wives;
But when old age crept over them,
  With many, many qualms,
King Solomon wrote the Proverbs
  And King David wrote the Psalms.

James Ball Naylor

*

THE GREAT AUK'S GHOST

The Great Auk's ghost rose on one leg,
  Sighed thrice and three times winkt,
And turned and poached a phantom egg,
  And muttered, 'I'm extinct.'

Ralph Hodgson

*

LITTLE WILLIE

Little Willie from his mirror
  Licked the mercury right off,
Thinking, in his childish error,
  It would cure the whooping cough.

At the funeral his mother
   Smartly said to Mrs. Brown:
'Twas a chilly day for Willie
When the mercury went down.'

Anon.

*

APPRECIATION

Auntie, did you feel no pain
Falling from that willow tree?
Will you do it, please, again?
'Cos my friend here didn't see.

Harry Graham

*

BIOGRAPHY FOR BEGINNERS

GEORGE HIRST

When I faced the bowling of Hirst
I ejaculated, 'Do your worst!'
He said, 'Right you are, Sid.'
– And he did.

LORD CLIVE

What I like about Clive
Is that he is no longer alive.
There is a great deal to be said
For being dead.

PROFESSOR JAMES DEWAR, F.R.S.

Professor Dewar
Is a better man than you are.
None of you assess
Can condense gases.

E.C. Bentley

MISS BUSS AND MISS BEALE

Miss Buss and Miss Beale
Cupid's darts do not feel.
How different from us
Miss Beale and Miss Buss.

Anon.

*

LATIN FOR TO-DAY

Latin is a dead tongue,
Dead as dead can be.
First it killed the Romans —
Now it's killing me.

Anon.

*

PREDESTINATION

There was a young man who said, 'Damn!
At last I've found out that I am —
A creature that moves
In determinate grooves,
In fact not a bus but a tram.'

Anon.

*

IDEALISM

There once was a man who said 'God
Must think it exceedingly odd
If he finds that this tree
Continues to be
When there's no one about in the Quad.'

Anon.(attr. to R A Knox)

ANSWER

Dear Sir, Your astonishment's odd:
I am always about in the Quad.
    And that's why the tree
    Will continue to be,
Since observed by Yours faithfully, God.

Anon.

*

THE KISS

'I saw you take his kiss!' 'Tis true,'
'O, modesty!' ''Twas strictly kept:
He thought me asleep: at least, I knew
He thought I thought he thought I slept.'

Coventry Patmore

*

ON THE MASTER OF BALLIOL

First come I; my name is Jowett.
There is no knowledge but I know it.
I am Master of this college:
What I don't know isn't knowledge.

Anon

*

TRIOLET

    I intended an Ode,
    And it turn'd to a Sonnet
    It began *à la mode*,
    I intended an Ode;
    But Rose cross'd the road
        In her latest new bonnet;
    I intended an Ode;
        And it turn'd to a Sonnet.

Austin Dobson

EPIGRAM

On parent knees, a naked new-born child,
Weeping thou sat'st while all around thee smiled:
So live, that, sinking in thy life's last sleep,
Calm thou may'st smile, while all around thee weep.

Sir William Jones

AN EPITAPH

Enough; and leave the rest to Fame;
'Tis to commend her, but to name.
Courtship which, living, she declined,
When dead, to offer were unkind.
Where never any could speak ill,
Who would officious praises spill?
Nor can the truest wit, or friend,
Without detracing, her commend.
To say — she lived a virgin chaste
In this age loose and all unlaced;
Nor was, when vice is so allowed,
Of virtue or ashamed or proud;
That her soul was on Heaven so bent,
No minute but it came and went;
That, ready her last debt to pay,
She summ'd her life up every day;
Modest as morn, as mid-day bright,
Gentle as evening, cool as night:
'Tis true; but all too weakly said;
'Twas more significant, she's dead.

Andrew Marvell

UPON THE DEATH OF SIR ALBERT MORTON'S WIFE

He first deceased; she for a little tried
To live without him, liked it not, and died.

Sir Henry Wotton

ON THE UNIVERSITY CARRIER

*Who sickened in the time of his Vacancy, being
forbid to go to London by reason of the Plague.*

Here lies old Hobson. Death hath broke his girt,
And here, alas! hath laid him in the dirt;
Or else, the ways being foul, twenty to one
He's here stuck in a slough, and overthrown.
'Twas such a shifter that, if truth were known,
Death was half glad when he had got him down;
For he had any time this ten years full
Dodged with him betwixt Cambridge and *The Bull.*
And surely Death could never have prevailed,
Had not his weekly course of carriage failed;
But lately, finding him so long at home,
And thinking now his journey's end was come,
And that he had ta'en up his latest inn,
In the kind office of a chamberlin
Showed him his room where he must lodge that night,
Pulled off his boots, and took away the light.
If any ask for him, it shall be said,
'Hobson has supped, and's newly gone to bed.'

John Milton

'UNDERNEATH THIS SABLE HERSE'

Underneath this sable herse
Lies the subject of all verse:
Sidney's sister, Pembroke's mother:
Death, ere thou hast slain another
Fair and learn'd and good as she,
Time shall throw a dart at thee.

William Browne

EPITAPH ON SALATHIEL PAVY
A Child Of Queen Elizabeth's Chapel

Weep with me, all you that read
   This little story;
And know, for whom a tear you shed,
   Death's self is sorry.
'Twas a child, that so did thrive
   In grace, and feature,
As *Heaven* and *Nature* seem'd to strive
   Which own'd the creature.
Years he numbered scarce thirteen
   When *Fates* turn'd cruel,
Yet three fill'd *Zodiacks* had he been
   The stage's jewel;
And did act (what now we moan)
   Old men so duly,
As, sooth, the *Parcæ* thought him one,
   He play'd so truly.
So, by error, to his fate
   They all consented;
But viewing him since (alas, too late)
   They have repented.
And have sought (to give new birth)
   In baths to steep him;
But, being so much too good for earth,
   Heaven vows to keep him.

Ben Jonson

EPITAPH ON SIR EDWARD GILES AND HIS WIFE

No trust to metals nor to marbles, when
These have their fate and wear away as men;
Times, titles, trophies may be lost and spent,
But virtue rears the eternal monument.
What more than these can tombs or tombstones pay?
But here's the sunset of a tedious day:
These two asleep are: I'll but be undress'd
And so to bed: pray wish us all good rest.

Robert Herrick

ELGIN CATHEDRAL EPITAPH

Here lie I, Martin Elginbrodde:
Ha'e mercy o' my soul, Lord God,
As I wad do, were I Lord God
And ye were Martin Elginbrodde.

Anon.

JOHN BUN

Here lies John Bun,
He was killed by a gun,
His name was not Bun, but Wood,
But Wood would not rhyme with gun, but Bun would.

Anon.

IN A STAFFORDSHIRE CHURCHYARD

Here lies father and mother and sister and I,
    We all died within the space of one short year;
They all be buried at Wimble, except I,
    And I be buried here.

Anon.

Epitaph to THOMAS THETCHER
a Grenadier in the North Regt. of Hants Militia
who died of a violent Fever contracted by drinking
Small Beer when hot the 12th of May 1764

Here sleeps in peace a Hampshire Grenadier,
Who caught his death by drinking cold small Beer,
Soldiers be wise from his untimely fall
And when ye're hot drink Strong or none at all.
An honest Soldier never is forgot
Whether he die by Musket or by Pot.

Winchester Cathedral Graveyard

'THE SILVER SWAN'

The silver swan, who living had no note,
When death approached unlocked her silent throat;
Leaning her breast against the reedy shore,
Thus sung her first and last, and sung no more:
Farewell, all joys; O death, come close mine eyes;
More geese than swans now live, more fools than wise.

Orlando Gibbons

15
THE VISION SPLENDID

I saw Eternity the other night
VAUGHAN

THE RETREAT

Happy those early days, when I
Shin'd in my Angel-infancy!
Before I understood this place
Appointed for my second race,
Or taught my soul to fancy aught
But a white celestial thought:
When yet I had not walk'd above
A mile or two from my first Love,
And looking back — at that short space —
Could see a glimpse of His bright face:
When on some gilded cloud, or flow'r,
My gazing soul would dwell an hour,
And in those weaker glories spy
Some shadows of eternity:
Before I taught my tongue to wound
My Conscience with a sinful sound,
Or had the black art to dispense
A several sin to ev'ry sense,
But felt through all this fleshly dress
Bright shoots of everlastingness.

O how I long to travel back,
And tread again that ancient track!
That I might once more reach that plain
Where first I left my glorious train;
From whence th'enlightened spirit sees
That shady City of Palm-trees.
But ah! my soul with too much stay
Is drunk, and staggers in the way!
Some men a forward motion love,
But I by backward steps would move;
And when this dust falls to the urn,
In that state I came, return.

Henry Vaughan

322

VERTUE

Sweet day, so cool, so calm, so bright,
The bridall of the earth and skie,
The dew shall weep thy fall to-night;
    For thou must die.

Sweet rose, whose hue angrie and brave
Bids the rash gazer wipe his eye,
Thy root is ever in its grave,
    And thou must die.

Sweet spring, full of sweet days and roses,
A box where sweets compacted lie,
My musick shows ye have your closes,
    And all must die.

Only a sweet and vertuous soul,
Like season'd timber, never gives;
But though the whole world turn to coal,
    Then chiefly lives.

George Herbert

'AT THE ROUND EARTH'S IMAGINED CORNERS BLOW'

At the round earth's imagined corners blow
    Your trumpets, angels, and arise, arise
    From death, you numberless infinities
Of souls, and to your scattered bodies go:
All whom the flood did, and fire shall o'erthrow,
    All whom war, dearth, age, agues, tyrannies,
    Despair, law, chance hath slain, and you whose eyes
Shall behold God, and never taste death's woe.
But let them sleep, Lord, and me mourn a space,
    For if above all these my sins abound,

'Tis late to ask abundance of thy grace
   When we are there. Here on this lowly ground
      Teach me how to repent: for that's as good
      As if thou hadst sealed my pardon with thy blood.

John Donne

THE KINGDOM OF GOD

O world invisible, we view thee,
O world intangible, we touch thee,
O world unknowable, we know thee,
Inapprehensible, we clutch thee!

Does the fish soar to find the ocean,
The eagle plunge to find the air —
That we ask of the stars in motion
If they have rumour of thee there?

Not where the wheeling systems darken,
And our benumbed conceiving soars! —
The drift of pinions, would we hearken,
Beats at our own clay-shuttered doors.

The angels keep their ancient places; —
Turn but a stone, and start a wing!
'Tis ye, 'tis your estrangèd faces,
That miss the many-splendoured thing.

But (when so sad thou canst not sadder)
Cry; — and upon thy so sore loss
Shall shine the traffic of Jacob's ladder
Pitched betwixt Heaven and Charing Cross.

Yea, in the night, my Soul, my daughter,
Cry, — clinging Heaven by the hems;
And lo, Christ walking on the water
Not of Gennesareth, but Thames!

Francis Thompson

NEWS

News from a foreign Country came,
As if my Treasures and my Joys lay there;
So much it did my Heart enflame,
'Twas wont to call my Soul into mine Ear;
    Which thither went to meet
        Th' approaching Sweet,
    And on the Threshold stood
To entertain the secret Good;
        It hover'd there,
    As if 'twould leave mine Ear,
And was so eager to embrace
Th' expected Tidings, as they came,
That it could change its dwelling-place
    To entertain the same.

As if the Tidings were the Things
My very joys themselves, my foreign treasure,
    Or else did bear them on their wings,
With so much Joy they came, with so much Pleasure,
    My Soul stood at the Gate
        To recreate
    Itself with Bliss; and to
Be pleased with speed. A fuller view
        It fain would take,
    Yet Journeys back would make
Unto my heart, as if 'twould fain
Go out to meet, yet stay within,
Fitting a place to Entertain
    And bring the Tidings in.

What Sacred Instinct did inspire
My Soul in Childhood with an hope so strong?
    What secret Force mov'd my Desire
T' expect my Joys beyond the Seas, so Young?
        FELICITY I knew
            Was out of view;
        And being here alone,

I thought all Happiness was gone
    From Earth: for this
  I thirsted Absent Bliss,
Deeming that sure beyond the Seas,
Or else in something near at hand
I knew not yet (since nought did please
  I knew) my Bliss did stand.

  But little did the Infant dream
That all the Treasures of the World were by,
  And that Himself was so the Cream
  And Crown of all which round about did lye.
    Yet thus it was! The Gem,
      The Diadem,
    The Ring Enclosing all
That stood upon this Earthen Ball;
    The heav'nly Eye,
   Much wider than the Sky,
Wherein they All included were;
The Glorious Soul, that was the King
Made to possess them, did appear
  A Small and little Thing!

Thomas Traherne

IN TIME OF PESTILENCE
1593

Adieu, farewell earth's bliss!
This world uncertain is:
Fond are life's lustful joys,
Death proves them all but toys.
None from his darts can fly;
I am sick, I must die —
  Lord, have mercy on us!

Rich men, trust not in wealth,
Gold cannot buy you health;
Physic himself must fade;
All things to end are made;
The plague full swift goes by;
I am sick, I must die —
    Lord, have mercy on us!

Beauty is but a flower
Which wrinkles will devour;
Brightness falls from the air;
Queens have died young and fair;
Dust hath closed Helen's eye;
I am sick, I must die —
    Lord, have mercy on us!

Strength stoops unto the grave,
Worms feed on Hector brave;
Swords may not fight with fate;
Earth still holds ope her gate;
Come, come! the bells do cry;
I am sick, I must die —
    Lord, have mercy on us!

Wit with his wantonness
Tasteth death's bitterness;
Hell's executioner
Hath no ears for to hear
What vain art can reply;
I am sick, I must die —
    Lord, have mercy on us!

Haste therefore each degree
To welcome destiny;
Heaven is our heritage,
Earth but a player's stage.
Mount we unto the sky;
I am sick, I must die —
    Lord, have mercy on us!
                                Thomas Nashe

PREPARATIONS
(From the Christchurch MS.)

Yet if His Majesty, our sovereign lord,
Should of his own accord
Friendly himself invite,
And say 'I'll be your guest to-morrow night,'
How should we stir ourselves, call and command
All hands to work! 'Let no man idle stand!

'Set me fine Spanish tables in the hall;
See they be fitted all;
Let there be room to eat
And order taken that there want no meat.
See every sconce and candlestick made bright,
That without tapers they may give a light.

'Look to the presence: are the carpets spread,
The dazie o'er the head,
The cushions in the chairs,
And all the candles lighted on the stairs?
Perfume the chambers, and in any case
Let each man give attendance in his place!'

Thus, if a king were coming, would we do;
And 'twere good reason too;
For 'tis a duteous thing
To show all honour to an earthly king,
And after all our travail and our cost,
So he be pleased, to think no labour lost.

But at the coming of the King of Heaven
All's set at six and seven;
We wallow in our sin,
Christ cannot find a chamber in the inn.
We entertain Him always like a stranger,
And, as at first, still lodge Him in the manger.

Anon.

JORDAN

Who says that fictions onely and false hair
Become a verse? Is there in truth no beautie?
Is all good structure in a winding-stair?
May no lines passe, except they do their dutie
  Not to a true, but painted chair?

Is it no verse, except enchanted groves
And sudden arbours shadow course-spunne lines?
Must purling streams refresh a lover's loves?
Must all be vail'd while he that reades divines,
  Catching the sense at two removes?

Shepherds are honest people, let them sing:
Riddle who list, for me, and pull for prime,
I envie no man's nightingale or spring;
Nor let them punish me with loss of rhyme,
  Who plainly say, My God, my King.

George Herbert

THE CORONET

When for the thorns with which I long, too long,
  With many a piercing wound,
  My Saviour's head have crowned,
I seek with garlands to redress that wrong —
  Through every garden, every mead,
I gather flowers (my fruits are only flowers),
  Dismantling all the fragrant towers
That once adorned my shepherdess's head:
And now, when I have summed up all my store,
  Thinking (so I myself deceive)
  So rich a chaplet thence to weave

329

As never yet the King of Glory wore,
   Alas! I find the Serpent old,
   That, twining in his speckled breast,
   About the flowers disguised, does fold
   With wreaths of fame and interest.
Ah, foolish man, that wouldst debase with them,
And mortal glory, Heaven's diadem!
But thou who only couldst the Serpent tame,
Either his slippery knots at once untie,
And disentangle all his winding snare,
Or shatter too with him my curious frame,
And let these wither — so that he may die —
Though set with skill, and chosen out with care;
That they, while thou on both their spoils dost tread,
May crown Thy feet, that could not crown Thy head.

Andrew Marvell

WHEN THE WORLD IS BURNING

When the world is burning,
Fired within, yet turning
   Round with face unscathed;
Ere fierce flames, uprushing,
O'er all lands leap, crushing,
   Till earth fall, fire-swathed;
Up amidst the meadows,
Gently through the shadows,
   Gentle flames will glide,
Small, and blue, and golden,
Though by bard beholden,
When in calm dreams folden, —
   Calm his dreams will bide.

330

Where the dance is sweeping,
Through the greensward peeping,
   Shall the soft lights start;
Laughing maids, unstaying,
Deeming it trick-playing,
High their robes upswaying,
   O'er the lights shall dart;
And the woodland haunter
Shall not cease to saunter
   When, far down some glade,
Of the great world's burning,
One soft flame upturning
Seems, to his discerning,
   Crocus in the shade.

Ebenezer Jones

LAST LINES

No coward soul is mine,
No trembler in the world's storm-troubled sphere:
   I see Heaven's glories shine,
And faith shines equal, arming me from fear.

   O God within my breast,
Almighty, ever-present Deity!
   Life — that in me has rest,
As I — undying Life — have power in Thee!

   Vain are the thousand creeds
That move men's hearts: unutterably vain;
   Worthless as wither'd weeds,
Or idlest froth amid the boundless main,

   To waken doubt in one
Holding so fast by Thine infinity;

So surely anchor'd on
The steadfast rock of immortality.

With wide-embracing love
Thy Spirit animates eternal years,
  Pervades and broods above,
Changes, sustains, dissolves, creates, and rears.

Though earth and man were gone,
And suns and universes cease to be,
  And Thou were left alone,
Every existence would exist in Thee.

There is not room for Death,
Nor atom that his might could render void:
  Thou — Thou art Being and Breath,
And what Thou art may never be destroyed.

Emily Brontë

From 'KING LEAR'

Cordelia: ... We are not the first
Who with best meaning have incurred the worst.
For thee, oppressèd King, I am cast down;
Myself could else out-frown false Fortune's frown.
Shall we not see these daughters and these sisters?
Lear: No, no, no, no! Come, let's away to prison:
We two alone will sing like birds i'th'cage;
When thou dost ask me blessing, I'll kneel down
And ask of thee forgiveness. So we'll live,
And pray, and sing, and tell old tales, and laugh
At gilded butterflies, and hear poor rogues
Talk of court news; and we'll talk with them too —
Who loses and who wins, who's in, who's out —
And take upon's the mystery of things,
As if we were God's spies; and we'll wear out,
In a walled prison, packs and sects of great ones
That ebb and flow by th' moon.

William Shakespeare

ARBOR VITAE

For grace in me divined
This metaphor I find:
A tree.
    How can that be?

This tree all winter through
Found no green work to do —
No life
    Therein ran rife.

But with an awoken year
What surge of sap is here —
What flood
    In branch and bud.

So grace in me can hide —
Be darkened and denied —
Then once again
    Vesture my every vein.

Siegfried Sassoon

THE COLLAR

I struck the board, and cry'd, 'No more;
    I will abroad.'
What, shall I ever sigh and pine?
My lines and life are free; free as the road,
    Loose as the winde, as large as store.
        Shall I be still in suit?
Have I no harvest but a thorn
To let me bloud, and not restore
What I have lost with cordiall fruit?

333

Sure there was wine
Before my sighs did drie it; there was corn
Before my tears did drown it;
Is the yeare onely lost to me?
Have I no bayes to crown it,
No flowers, no garlands gay? all blasted,
All wasted?
No so, my heart; but there is fruit,
And thou hast hands.
Recover all thy sigh-blown age
On double pleasures; leave thy cold dispute
Of what is fit and not; forsake thy cage,
Thy rope of sands
Which pettie thoughts have made; and made to thee
Good cable, to enforce and draw,
And be thy law,
While thou didst wink and wouldst not see.
Away! take heed;
I will abroad.
Call in thy death's-head there, tie up thy fears;
He that forbears
To suit and serve his need
Deserves his load.
But as I rav'd and grew more fierce and wilde
At every word,
Methought I heard one calling, 'Childe';
And I reply'd, 'My Lord.'

George Herbert

From 'INTIMATIONS OF IMMORTALITY'

O joy! that in our embers
Is something that doth live,
That nature yet remembers
What was so fugitive!

The thought of our past years in me doth breed
Perpetual benediction: not indeed
For that which is most worthy to be blest —
Delight and liberty, the simple creed
Of Childhood, whether busy or at rest,
With new-fledged hope still fluttering in his breast:-
  Not for these I raise
  The song of thanks and praise;
 But for those obstinate questionings
 Of sense and outward things,
 Fallings from us, vanishings;
 Blank misgivings of a Creature
Moving about in worlds not realised,
High instincts before which our mortal Nature
Did tremble like a guilty Thing surprised:
  But for those first affections,
  Those shadowy recollections,
 Which, be they what they may,
Are yet the fountain light of all our day,
Are yet a master light of all our seeing;
 Uphold us, cherish, and have power to make
Our noisy years seem moments in the being
Of the eternal Silence: truths that wake,
  To perish never;
Which neither listlessness, nor mad endeavour,
  Nor Man nor Boy,
Nor all that is at enmity with joy,
Can utterly abolish or destroy!
  Hence in a season of calm weather
  Though inland far we be,
Our Souls have sight of that immortal sea
  Which brought us hither,
  Can in a moment travel thither,
And see the Children sport upon the shore,
And hear the mighty waters rolling evermore.

         William Wordsworth

THE REVIVAL

Unfold! unfold! Take in His light,
Who makes thy cares more short than night.
The joys which with His day-star rise
He deals to all but drowsy eyes;
And, what the men of this world miss,
Some drops and dews of future bliss.

Hark! how His winds have chang'd their note!
And with warm whispers call thee out;
The frosts are past, the storms are gone,
And backward life at last comes on.
The lofty groves in express joys
Reply unto the turtle's voice;
And here in dust and dirt, O here
The lilies of His love appear!

Henry Vaughan

LOVE

Love bade me welcome; yet my soul drew back,
   Guilty of dust and sin.
But quick-eyed Love, observing me grow slack
   From my first entrance in,
Drew nearer to me, sweetly questioning
   If I lack'd anything.

'A guest,' I answer'd, 'worthy to be here:'
   Love said, 'You shall be he.'
'I, the unkind, ungrateful? Ah, my dear,
   I cannot look on Thee.'
Love took my hand, and smiling did reply,
   'Who made the eyes but I?'

336

'Truth, Lord; but I have marr'd them; let my shame
  Go where it doth deserve.'
'And know you not,' says Love, 'Who bore the blame?'
  'My dear, then I will serve.'
'You must sit down,' says Love, 'and taste my Meat.'
  So I did sit and eat.

George Herbert

THE HABIT OF PERFECTION

Elected Silence, sing to me
And beat upon my whorlèd ear,
Pipe me to pastures still and be
The music that I care to hear.

Shape nothing, lips; be lovely-dumb:
It is the shut, the curfew sent
From there where all surrenders come
Which only makes you eloquent.

Be shellèd, eyes, with double dark
And find the uncreated light:
This ruck and reel which you remark
Coils, keeps, and teases simple sight.

Palate, the hutch of tasty lust,
Desire not to be rinsed with wine:
The can must be so sweet, the crust
So fresh that come in fasts divine!

Nostrils, your careless breath that spend
Upon the stir and keep of pride,
What relish shall the censers send
Along the sanctuary side!

O feel-of-primrose hands, O feet
That want the yield of plushy award,
But you shall walk the golden street
And you unhouse and house the Lord.

And, Poverty, be thou the bride
And now the marriage feast begun,
And lily-coloured clothes provide
Your spouse not laboured-at nor spun.

Gerard Manley Hopkins

ULYSSES

It little profits that an idle king,
By this still hearth, among these barren crags,
Match'd with an aged wife, I mete and dole
Unequal laws unto a savage race,
That hoard, and sleep, and feed, and know not me.
I cannot rest from travel: I will drink
Life to the lees: all times I have enjoy'd
Greatly, have suffer'd greatly, both with those
That loved me, and alone; on shore, and when
Thro' scudding drifts the rainy Hyades
Vext the dim sea: I am become a name;
For always roaming with a hungry heart
Much have I seen and known; cities of men
And manners, climates, councils, governments,
Myself not least, but honour'd of them all;
And drunk delight of battle with my peers,
Far on the ringing plains of windy Troy.
I am a part of all that I have met;
Yet all exprience is an arch wherethro'
Gleams that untravell'd world, whose margin fades
For ever and for ever when I move.
How dull it is to pause, to make an end,
To rust unburnish'd, not to shine in use!

As tho' to breathe were life. Life piled on life
Were all too little, and of one to me
Little remains: but every hour is saved
From that eternal silence, something more,
A bringer of new things; and vile it were
For some three suns to store and hoard myself,
And this gray spirit yearning in desire
To follow knowledge like a sinking star,
Beyond the utmost bound of human thought.
    This is my son, mine own Telemachus,
To whom I leave the sceptre and the isle —
Well-loved of me, discerning to fulfil
This labour, by slow prudence to make mild
A rugged people, and thro' soft degrees
Subdue them to the useful and the good.
Most blameless is he, centred in the sphere
Of common duties, decent not to fail
In offices of tenderness, and pay
Meet adoration to my household gods,
When I am gone. He works his work, I mine.
    There lies the port; the vessel puffs her sail:
There gloom the dark broad seas. My mariners,
Souls that have toil'd, and wrought, and thought with me —
That ever with a frolic welcome took
The thunder and the sunshine, and opposed
Free hearts, free foreheads — you and I are old;
Old age hath yet his honour and his toil;
Death closes all: but something ere the end,
Some work of noble note, may yet be done,
Not unbecoming men that strove with Gods.
The lights begin to twinkle from the rocks:
The long day wanes: the slow moon climbs: the deep
Moans round with many voices. Come, my friends,
'Tis not too late to seek a newer world.
Push off, and sitting well in order smite
The sounding furrows; for my purpose holds
To sail beyond the sunset, and the baths
Of all the western stars, until I die.

It may be that the gulfs will wash us down:
It may be we shall touch the Happy Isles,
And see the great Achilles, whom we knew.
Tho' much is taken, much abides; and tho'
We are not now that strength which in old days
Moved earth and heaven; that which we are, we are;
One equal temper of heroic hearts,
Made weak by time and fate, but strong in will
To strive, to seek, to find, and not to yield.

Alfred Tennyson

EASTER HYMN

Death and darkness, get you packing,
Nothing now to man is lacking;
All your triumphs now are ended,
And what Adam marr'd is mended;
Graves are beds now for the weary,
Death a nap, to wake more merry;
Youth now, full of pious duty,
Seeks in Thee for perfect beauty;
The weak and aged, tir'd with length
Of days, from Thee look for new strength;
And infants with Thy pangs contest
As pleasant as if with the breast.
   Then, unto Him, Who thus hath thrown
Even to contempt thy kingdom down,
And by His blood did us advance
Unto His own inheritance;
To Him be glory, power, praise,
From this unto the last of days!

Henry Vaughan

THE ARGUMENT OF HIS BOOK

I sing of brooks, of blossoms, birds and bowers,
Of April, May, of June and July-flowers;
I sing of May-poles, hock-carts, wassails, wakes,
Of bridegrooms, brides and of their bridal cakes;
I write of youth, of love, and have access
By these to sing of cleanly wantonness;
I sing of dews, of rains, and piece by piece
Of balm, of oil, of spice and ambergris;
I sing of times trans-shifting, and I write
How roses first came red and lilies white;
I write of groves, of twilights, and I sing
The Court of Mab, and of the Fairy King;
I write of hell; I sing (and ever shall)
Of heaven, and hope to have it after all.

Robert Herrick

343

344

INDEX OF FIRST LINES

347